CATHOLICISM *and* SCOTLAND

THE VOICE OF SCOTLAND

*A List of Volumes
in the series:*

CATHOLICISM
and SCOTLAND

by

COMPTON MACKENZIE

GEORGE ROUTLEDGE
AND SONS, LTD. Broadway
House, Carter Lane, London, E.C.
1936

PRINTED IN GREAT BRITAIN BY THE EDINBURGH PRESS, EDINBURGH AND LONDON

IN MEMORIAM

J. LESLIE MITCHELL
(Lewis Grassic Gibbon)

Death hath this also : that it openeth the
gate to good fame, and extinguisheth envy.

BACON.

CONTENTS

AUTHOR'S NOTE

THIS book was written at the suggestion of the late
J. Leslie Mitchell. Unwilling to involve myself in
the odium of religious controversy, I wished to
substitute Jacobitism for Catholicism, and thus the
matter was arranged. One day, several months later,
I felt suddenly impelled to return to the original
suggestion and immediately notified Mitchell of my
change of mind. I was too late. He was already
dead when my letter was posted to him. A melancholy
coincidence, no doubt, and nothing more; but as
some of Mitchell's friends might suppose *Catholicism
and Scotland* an inappropriate book to dedicate to the
memory of this writer whose untimely death has been
such a heavy loss to Scottish letters, I think it right to
append this note of explanation.

ISLE OF BARRA, 1935.

ix

CATHOLICISM AND SCOTLAND

CHAPTER I

" THE Celtic Church was one in faith with the rest
of Catholic Christendom, its system of worship, of
which the Eucharistic Sacrifice was the centre, was
based on principles common to the whole Church;
but it was not Roman in the sense of following the
liturgy, customs and usages of the local Roman
Church. In some respects it resembled the Uniate
Churches of the East at the present day which,
although in communion with Rome, preserve their
own discipline, liturgies and customs. Here, however,
the resemblance ceases, for the Celtic Church was part
of Latin Christendom."

Those words are quoted from an essay [1] by the
Reverend John Campbell MacNaught, B.D., Minister
of Kilmuir Easter, every page of which displays the
author as a scholar able and willing to subordinate
sectarian prejudice to historical truth.

It might have been hoped that with the publication
of this essay what Major M. V. Hay has called the

---

[1] *The Celtic Church and the See of Peter.* Blackwell.

Chain of Error in Scottish History had at last been finally broken, and that Presbyterians and Episcopalians would henceforth confine their apologetics to justifying the repudiation of Papal authority and primacy instead of attempting to prove that neither authority nor primacy had ever been admitted. Yet the Chain of Error still fetters Protestant apologists.

As recently as July 22nd, 1935, we find the Reverend Doctor A. J. Campbell, Clerk of the Presbytery of Glasgow, reported in the *Glasgow Herald* as saying in the course of an address at a conventicle on the Lammermoor hillside:

" When they thought of the monks of Soutra they thought of them not as Romanists but as Scotsmen, men of their own blood and of their own Church. When the Scottish Reformers carried through the Scottish Reformation they did not regard themselves as pulling down an old Church and setting up a new Church in its place. They regarded themselves as clearing out of the Scottish Church an alien, intrusive, injurious influence which had no business to be there. They reformed the Church, but after the process it was still the same Church."

We have long been accustomed to that fanciful conception of the past which was responsible for handing over Iona to the Established Church of Scotland in the belief that modern Presbyterianism was the religious body nearest in spirit to Saint Columba and his monks; but that will not content Dr Campbell. He must make good Covenanters of the Cistercians. Nor is this mere eccentricity. Claims not less wild may be read almost every day in the correspondence columns of the Scottish Press, and presumably they indicate what may often be heard from the pulpits.

In a recently published brief survey of Scottish history [1] Mr Colin Walkinshaw contends that "what St Columba's success did was not to give Scotland . . . a rival Church to the Roman Catholic, but to strengthen and confirm the Celtic civilization which was being established among the German tribes of the South." This is true up to a point, but it should be borne in mind that it was not so much the Latin civilization which was disliked as the channel through which it was flowing after the mission of Saint Augustine. Celtic Christianity was as truly Latin as that of Saint Augustine. In the famous letter of Saint Columbanus to Pope Boniface IV, the mutilation of an extract from which by Dr W. F. Skene proved such a booby-trap for the nineteenth-century historians who copied Dr Skene without consulting the original text, there is the clearest acknowledgment of Papal supremacy. This is how Major Hay, to whom is due

[1] *The Scots Tragedy*. Routledge.

3

the credit of having exposed a number of reputed historians, translates that extract : [1]

" For all we Irish living at the uttermost ends of the earth are the disciples of SS. Peter and Paul, and of all the disciples who wrote the sacred canon under the inspiration of the Holy Spirit; receiving nothing outside the evangelical and apostolical doctrine; no heretic, no Jew, no schismatic was ever amongst us; but the Catholic Faith as it was first delivered to us from you, the successors, that is, of the holy apostles, is retained amongst us unchanged."

The cutting off of the Celtic Church from communication with Rome by the invaders may have kept it out of touch with the rest of Christendom; but that temporary severance of communication did not mean a loss of communion, although Columbanus, who was a bitter supporter of the archaic Easter date which had probably been introduced into Britain by the British bishops that attended the Council of Arles of 314, might as the result of it be just three centuries behind the times.

This settlement of the date of Easter was not a trivial matter. The perpetual struggle of the Catholic Church for unity demanded uniformity, and inasmuch as the whole cycle of movable feasts throughout the

[1] *A Chain of Error in Scottish History.* By M. V. Hay. Longmans, p. 111.

liturgical year depended upon the date of Easter, the keeping of Easter at different dates struck as hard a blow as could be imagined at uniformity, and therefore at unity. In dread of Anglo-Saxon aggression the Celtic churchmen resisted every effort to persuade them to surrender their archaic usages and conform with the rest of Christendom. "Rome is in error," wrote Cummian ironically. "Jerusalem is in error. Antioch is in error. The whole world is in error. Only the Britons and the Scots possess the truth." Truly the child is father of the man.

Yet it is significant that, when the danger of absorption into the kingdom of Northumbria had vanished, the opposition to complete uniformity in all essentials with the rest of the Catholic Church vanished with it.

In 710, just twenty-five years after the defeat of Egfrith at the battle of Dunnichen or Nectansmere, Naiton, King of the Picts, compelled all the monks and clerics in his realm to come into line over the date of Easter. Monks in communion with Iona who still refused to conform were banished, seven years later, beyond the Grampians. There is no doubt that Naiton was as deeply impressed as Oswy of Northumbria had been half a century earlier by the citation of Saint Matthew's Gospel. *Thou art Peter and upon this rock I will build my Church, and the gates*

*of hell shall not prevail against it; and I will give thee
the keys of the kingdom of heaven.* Bede tells us that
Naiton placed his kingdom under the protection of
Saint Peter. It was probably not until the relics of
Saint Andrew were brought to Scotland, perhaps
from the Abbey of Hexham for safety from desecration
by the Norsemen, that Saint Peter ceased to be the
country's patron saint.

It is a habit of Protestant historians to qualify
the importance of such early recognition of Papal
supremacy by insisting that Papal supremacy meant
something different than from what it means now.
Yet meditation with even the most superficial attention
to logic upon these words recorded by Saint Matthew
should be enough to suggest that they must be applied
to the whole of time. If our Blessed Lord spoke these
words, Papal supremacy means now what it meant
at any date since they were uttered and what it
will mean at any date until the consummation of the
world. The Scottish or English Catholic may speculate
what effect on the popular religious notions of their
two countries has been produced by the impossibility
of translating our Lord's words adequately either into
English or into Gaelic. They were most conclusive
in the Aramaic of His very utterance. *Thou art
Cephas* (a rock) *and on this Cephas I will build my
Church.* In the Greek of the New Testament, in

the Latin of the Vulgate, in French and in Italian, and in so many other languages it is possible to give the full force of that tremendous assertion; but how is it to be conveyed in English or in Gaelic to the private interpreter of the Holy Scriptures, whose boasted privilege makes him suspicious even of a footnote's profane influence? *Gur tusa Peadar, agus air a charraig so togaidh mi m'Eaglais, 's cha toir geatachan ifrinn buaidh oirre.* How shall the devout Skyeman, reading the Gospel by the light of his own judgment, understand that " Peadar " and " carraig " are the same? Why from the reading of these words in his Gaelic Bible should the Skyeman be led to ask himself in a sudden humility whether, on that dim blue island thirty-five miles nearer to the setting sun, the Barraman might not have been granted by the Grace of God a revelation of the Divine purpose more illuminating than the feeble rushlight of his own intelligence?

It is not within the scope of this book to speculate what precisely that shadowy Pictish King in the stormy mists of the eighth century understood by his recognition of Papal supremacy; but it is essential to make it clear to the non-Catholic reader how firmly the author believes that such a recognition twelve hundred years ago or more must involve a spiritual enlightenment transcending what is called practical politics. It is not the jurisdiction itself which matters so much as the guarantee of truth which the recognition of that jurisdiction includes. What we know of the gradual emergence of the Scottish nation during the next three centuries and a half is very little, but at least we can affirm that the central truths of the Christian religion were never as fiercely threatened in Scotland throughout the monotonous violence of that epoch as they are threatened to-day by the intellectual despair and doctrinal anarchy to which Protestantism has reduced the country. " The work of the Spirit of holiness is hindered by our sinful divisions," writes [1] Mr MacNaught. " He is the Spirit of unity, the one Spirit who dwells in the One Body. An old Highlander, when his minister was speaking to him about the Church, exclaimed, ' *Eaglais! chan'eil ach bloighean de dh 'Eaglais againn.'* (' Church! We have only splinters of a Church.') The significance of the old man's exclamation will be appreciated when we consider that, in a sparsely populated parish, he had before his eyes the sad spectacle of four different Presbyterian Churches, whose members could not unite in partaking together of what each believed to be the great Sacrament of Christian fellowship."

Yet the glimpses we obtain from time to time of

[1] *The Celtic Church and the See of Peter*, p. 111.

ecclesiastical organization and discipline suggest that the long struggle to maintain the national entity in spite of devastating Norsemen and the internecine wars of dynastic rivalries had reduced the spiritual life to a very low ebb. Concubinage among the clergy with its attendant evil of hereditary succession to benefices was widespread. The Abbots of the great Columban monasteries were now mostly secular nobles, and the vital need of a Scotland which by the first quarter of the eleventh century, except for the islands and the extreme north-east of the mainland still in the hands of the Norwegians, had become the geographical Scotland of to-day was organized diocesan government and the final clearing up of the degenerate remains of Columban monasticism.

In 1069 the Bishop of St Andrews, the only bishop in the country, celebrated the nuptials of King Malcolm Canmore with Princess Margaret, the sister of Edgar Atheling, the granddaughter of Edmund Ironsides, and the grand-niece of Saint Edward the Confessor. It was a critical moment in the history of the Northern kingdom. Three years before, William of Normandy had set out on his conquest of England, and a struggle between Scotland and the Anglo-Norman realm he was to create was inevitable sooner or later. The alliance between the Scottish Royal House and the sister of the legitimist heir of the Saxon Royal House would give to the issue of such a marriage an unmistakable European royalty, and in no European state was the monarchy to become more definitely the symbol of the nation. The failure of the Irish Royal House to achieve a comparable status of royalty that was recognized beyond Ireland was not the least important of the causes that contributed to the success of the Angevin conquest in destroying the outward appearance of a nation, powerless though it may have been to damage the substance of nationality. Indeed the identification of the Scottish nation with the Scottish King, which lingers to-day in the popular esteem for the or and gules of the King's personal standard over the argent and azure of the saltire of Saint Andrew, was to end by being a positive danger to conscious nationality, and the vitality of the Irish nation in the twentieth century, which makes every Scots patriot blush with shame, may be partially ascribed to Ireland's lack of obligation to any king in the maintenance of that national spirit.

Margaret brought more than prestige to Scotland. She was a woman of intellect and breeding. She was a woman of indomitable will. She was a great practical organizer. She was a wonderful wife and a perfect mother. Above all she was a Saint.

We are fortunate enough to possess a brief but

illuminating life of the Queen almost certainly by her confessor, Turgot, that Prior of Durham who was afterwards to become Bishop of St Andrews, and we are therefore able to comprehend the full extent of her services to the country she made her own, besides recognizing in her a character of outstanding beauty and strength.

There is a generally diffused belief nowadays that Saint Margaret was primarily responsible for the extinction of the Gaelic language in the Lowlands of Scotland, and that it was she who started that nefarious business of trying to make Scotland Roman Catholic. There is no doubt that the Queen did take a strong line with her husband's Gaelic subjects, but it should be remembered that Malcolm himself was bilingual and just as anxious as his wife to keep them in order. The Gaelic sentimentalist must consider the alternative. If there had been no marriage between Malcolm and Margaret Scotland without any doubt would have been conquered by one of the successors of William of Normandy as Ireland was conquered by Henry II, but with this difference that the conquest of Scotland would have been so complete as to anticipate by several centuries that gradual absorption into England since the Act of Union. It is impossible to suppose that a purely Gaelic Scotland could have withstood for long the Anglo-Norman power of the South, and the argument that the chief factor in the success of the struggle for independence against the Edwards was the Celtic element takes insufficiently into account the importance of leadership. The paradox of the history of Great Britain and Ireland is that it requires a Celt to lead a Saxon and a Saxon to lead a Celt, or let us say more accurately a man with a non-Celtic background. It is equally impossible to suppose that the disorganized Scottish Church could have survived much longer without the reforming genius of Saint Margaret. The fact has to be faced that the Scottish Church was an anachronism in Christendom, not because it was apostolic or primitive or evangelical or protestant or anti-papal, but because it was barbaric and rapidly growing more barbaric.

The first irregularity the Queen adjusted was the Lenten fast. It was the custom in Scotland to begin the fast on the Monday after Ash Wednesday, and Margaret decided that the Celtic ecclesiastics should follow the rule of the rest of the Church in this regard. To the argument that on the authority of the Gospels our Lord fasted for six weeks Margaret replied that He fasted for forty days and that since the six Sundays were deducted the result in Scotland was a fast of thirty-six days. The Conservatives were persuaded, and the fast began henceforth on Ash Wednesday. This may not seem an important matter, but like that dispute about Easter four hundred years earlier, it involved the larger issue of unity through uniformity.

The second reform was graver. Margaret asked the Celtic churchmen to justify their habit of avoiding the Easter Communion and was told that they feared the words of Saint Paul about eating and drinking unworthily to their own damnation. The Queen pointed out that in the Sacrament of Penance the Church offered a guard against such a fearful retribution, and her argument was convincing. She also prevailed upon the Celtic churchmen to work for the abolition of certain " barbarous rites " in the celebration of masses.

What these barbarous rites were we have no idea. There are certainly no grounds whatever for presuming as some historians have presumed that it refers to saying Mass in Gaelic. Major Hay has pointed out [1] that this is a loose speculation by Skene which has been hastily accepted by later historians. He himself suggests that the allusion may be to some " primitive Gallican form elsewhere forgotten." It is, however, possible that pagan corruptions had crept in. We have evidence of the Gael's inclination to pagan rites as late as the sixteenth century, and that abstention from the Easter Communion suggests a widespread degeneration. Worthy Protestants have

[1] *A Chain of Error in Scottish History*, pp. 251-4.

13

discerned in it an early exhibition of the Calvinistic conscience inspired by the appeal to evangelical authority; but it is scarcely necessary to insist that what we do know about the Celtic Church forbids any such explanation.

The next fault the Queen had to find was with the habitual desecration of the Lord's Day by servile work. Apparently it was a tradition of the monastic Irish Church to rest from work on Saturday with the Jews and to observe Sunday merely as a religious festival, and there have not been wanting apologists to find this primitive observance an inspiration for the later extravagances of Sabbath worship in Scotland. It might be rash to presume that five centuries after the death of Columba Scottish churchmen were still keeping Saturday as a day of rest in preference. Yet it is difficult not to fancy that this custom still possessed a certain authority. At any rate, the Queen succeeded in impressing upon her husband's subjects the sanctity of Sunday, for we are told that they observed it henceforth with such strictness that nobody carried burdens himself on that day or required such labour from others.

Shall we trace to Saint Margaret the popularity of the Calvinistic Sunday? Or shall we say that the Scots are predisposed to keep the Sabbath? Indeed it may be so. Even the Catholic islanders who have never been affected by the Reformation are inclined to observe Sunday with more austerity than most Catholics, and among some of the older people there is an inclination to suppose that the latitude in the matter of recreation among the younger people is too wide; but it goes without saying that there is neither grimness nor gloom, and that the melancholic excesses of the Calvinistic Sabbath are unimaginable. The central fact of Sunday for a Catholic is that upon that day our Saviour rose from the dead and that in the Sunday Mass he must attend he celebrates that glorious Resurrection which assures himself of immortal life. It was of this central fact that Saint Margaret reminded the Scottish churchmen when she remonstrated with them for desecrating Sunday by servile labour. It was of the Presence of Jesus Christ upon their altars that she reminded them, of that Presence which was to be denied by the Reformers and by the denial of which they turned their Sabbath-worship into a mockery of Almighty God. To that we must return later. It is enough for now to insist that the Sunday for which Queen Margaret demanded due observance was the Sunday hallowed by the Resurrection of the Saviour, and that the observance she demanded for it was exactly the same as is demanded from the millions and millions of Catholics all over the world to-day.

Another abuse which Queen Margaret set out to

correct was that of marriages within the prohibited degrees; but her biographer is silent on the subject of the two greatest abuses of all, the concubinage of the clergy and the lay usurpation of church property and ecclesiastical office. Skene suggested as an explanation for this the consciousness of the Queen that her own husband was the descendant of a lay abbot and that one of her own young sons was lay Abbot of Dunkeld. However, if we have no record of any attempt by Queen Margaret to extirpate clerical concubinage, we do know that she went out of her way to show special favour to the many anchorites all over the country leading ascetic and holy lives. We know, too, that she rebuilt the mother house of Iona destroyed by the Norsemen and restored the monks. Whatever the Queen may have found to criticize in Celtic churchmanship, it was to the most essential values and the most characteristic aspects of Celtic churchmanship that her saintly mind turned for spiritual help.

In ~~1903~~, three days after her husband had perished by treachery in Northumberland, Queen Margaret died and was canonized by Innocent IV in 1250. Her feast is kept on White Rose Day, the tenth of June.[1] June is the month of Bannockburn, and we who still

[1] In Scotland itself, owing to St Columba's feast falling upon June 9th, her feast is kept on November 16th, the date of her death.

16

commemorate that victory should remember that if there had been no Saint Margaret to give Scotland kings like Alexander I and David I there would never have been a Bannockburn. It was the great work of consolidation effected by them which gave Scotland that awareness of herself as a nation to inspire and sustain the war of independence.

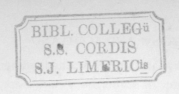
CHAPTER II

ALL ecclesiastical history involves paying so much
attention to ecclesiastical disputes as to make religion
an easy target for the cynic. Yet when these disputes
are examined it will usually be found that the causes
which provoked them were matters of vital principle.
Such a dispute was caused by the nomination of Queen
Margaret's biographer Turgot to the see of St Andrews,
which had been vacant for fourteen years when in
1107 Alexander I succeeded to the throne of Scotland.
The new King was determined to take advantage of
the state of the country, which was now settled after
the wars among the various claimants following the
death of Malcolm Canmore, to press on with his
mother's reformation of the Scottish Church, and
substitute for the archaic monastic rule that system of
diocesan and parochial organization now general in
Christendom. The nomination of Turgot to the see
of St Andrews resulted in a definite claim by the
Archbishop of York to jurisdiction over the Scottish
Church, based upon a letter from Pope Gregory the
Great to Saint Augustine, putting all British bishops

under his jurisdiction and at his death dividing them between the primates of Canterbury and York, each with twelve suffragans. The very existence of a Celtic Church was hardly apprehended in Rome when Augustine set out to convert the Angles.

Turgot's consecration to the vacant see was finally arranged by a compromise, but on his death in 1115 Alexander I tried to overleap the claims of York by obtaining Eadmer, a monk of Canterbury, for the vacant bishopric and demanding for him as an ancient right consecration either by the Pope or the Archbishop of Canterbury. This attempt to bring in Canterbury was a diplomatic trick to start a quarrel between the two English primates. Meanwhile, Alexander went ahead with his diocesan plans by creating the two sees of Moray and Dunkeld, thus indicating his intention of countering the Scandinavian influence in north-east Scotland, where another dispute was going on over the see of Orkney between the Archbishops of Hamburg and York, who both claimed jurisdiction.

Alexander died without the status of the see of St Andrews being decided. He was succeeded by his younger brother, David, who was equally zealous on behalf of the Scottish Church. Alexander had introduced the Austin Canons. David brought Benedictines from France to Selkirk. A more important step was the restoration of the see of Glasgow, over which York claimed supremacy. The new Bishop was called to Rome by Paschal II, consecrated by him, but put under obedience to the Metropolitan of York. Calixtus II confirmed his predecessor's ruling; but the Bishop of Glasgow continued to resist submission to the Archbishop of York. The dispute was not settled until 1188 when Pope Clement III declared the Scottish sees dependent immediately upon the Apostolic See and independent of any other, a full recognition of the work of Alexander and David, the latter of whom had added the bishoprics of Ross, Aberdeen, Caithness, Dunblane, and Brechin to Glasgow, besides many great religious foundations—Benedictine, Cistercian, Praemonstratensian and Augustinian.

What this declaration of Clement III meant to the Scottish nation may be judged by the state of affairs after the Treaty of Falaise in 1174 when William the Lion, to obtain his freedom, bound himself to do homage to the King of England as his feudal superior. In that treaty the King of England provided also for the superiority of the English Metropolitan over the Scottish Church. Two years later the Papal Legate summoned a council at Northampton, at which Henry II of England demanded a formal acknowledgment from the Scottish bishops of their subjection to the English Church. In argument with the Archbishop of York the Bishop of Glasgow claimed that his see was "the special daughter of the Roman Church, and exempt from all subjection to archbishops." This claim was recognized by Pope Alexander III in 1178, and to-day the archiepiscopal see of Glasgow is directly under the Apostolic See. At Northampton the proceedings were complicated by the Archbishop of Canterbury's claim that his own see was supreme over the Scottish Church and not that of his colleague of York. The Council broke up without deciding this new problem of jurisdiction, and for the next decade the struggle for the freedom of the Scottish Church from English supremacy was prolonged. Then on March 13, 1188, by the Bull *Cum Universi* the Scottish Church was made immediately subject to Rome. Nobody except the Pope or his legate was to pronounce sentence of interdict or excommunication in Scotland. Questions over Church property were not to be decided in Scotland except by appeal to Rome. Nobody except a Scotsman unless specially sent from Rome should exercise the office of legate in Scotland. In the following year Richard Cœur de Lion, wanting money for the Third Crusade, annulled the Treaty of Falaise for 10,000 marks, and by another treaty signed at Canterbury on December 5th, 1189, the spiritual and temporal independence of Scotland was solemnly accepted. Thus we see that what the Reverend Dr A. J. Campbell calls an "alien, intrusive, injurious influence" turns out to be the prime influence on behalf of Scottish freedom.

In 1200 John, Bishop of Dunkeld, who was ignorant of Gaelic, petitioned the Pope to divide his see and appoint to the new see carved out of it his chaplain Harold who did speak Gaelic. Are we to believe the Celtic sentimentalists who claim that Saint Margaret was responsible for the extirpation of Gaelic from the south? Could the language really have been so widespread if it had vanished in a hundred years? Surely it is clear that the Gaelic-speaking districts were in 1200 the north and the west even as in a sadly diluted way they remain the Gaelic-speaking districts to-day. The Bishop of Dunkeld's care for his Gaelic flock is a certain indication. So scrupulous a man would have resigned from his whole diocese if the half he retained had been Gaelic. The Pope himself consecrated Harold to be the first Bishop of Argyll and much commended the generosity and Christian fervour of the Bishop of Dunkeld who was endowing the new and exclusively Gaelic see from his own revenues. The Cathedral was built on the island of Lismore. Soon after this at the prompting of Ronald, the son of Somerled, Lord of the Isles, Benedictine monks took over Iona from the Culdees, a step which in Skene's opinion marked the definite end of the old Celtic Church.

English claims were asserted again in 1249 when Henry III, on hearing of the death of Alexander II of Scotland, petitioned Pope Innocent IV to forbid the coronation of the eight-year-old heir, Alexander III, without the consent of the English monarch, at the same time demanding the tithe of all benefices in Scotland. To both requests the Pope returned a flat refusal, and no more was heard of the matter for another fifty years.

During the thirteenth century Scotland marched in step with that sublime procession of the Middle Ages toward eternity, and the century of peace with England was the outward sign of that accord. There is a legend that Alexander III became a friend of Saint Dominic in Paris. Be that as it may, he had a particular devotion for the great Order of Preachers, and founded eight houses, including one at Inverness which was a powerful educational influence in the north. Two Franciscan foundations were established also. The Doctor Subtilis, Duns Scotus, is claimed as a son of Saint Francis, and he is reputed to have been the most brilliant exponent of the doctrine of the Immaculate Conception in the University of Paris, the centre of the logical opposition to that Oxford advocacy of which Duns Scotus was the champion.

23

The long reign of Alexander III came to a premature end on that sixteenth of March which Thomas the Rhymer prophesied should be the stormiest day Scotland had ever known. He was riding along the sea-coast of Fife to meet his bride of the year before, Yolanda of Dreux, whom he had married after the loss of his first wife Margaret, the daughter of Henry III of England, in the hope of a male heir. In the year 1285 his horse stumbled and threw him over a rock to death when he was still in his prime.

The loss to Scotland was beyond reckoning. He left only a girl child to succeed him, his grand-daughter, the Maid of Norway. A shudder of dread shook the country.

> Quhen Alysandyr, oure king, wes dede,
> That Scotland led in luwe (love) and le (peace),
> Away wes sons of ale and brede,
> Of wyne and wax, of gamyn and gle.
> Our gold wes changyd into lede (grief).
> Christ, born into virgynyte,
> Succour Scotland, and remede
> That stad (placed) is in perplexyte.

It is pathetically typical of poor Sir Walter Scott's dense ignorance of Catholicism that out of a kind of religious prudery he should maltreat that poignant cry of the poet's thus:

" When Alexander our King was dead,
   Who Scotland led in love and le,
Away was wealth of ale and bread,
   Of wine and wax, of game and glee.
Then pray to God, since only he
   Can succour Scotland in her need,
That placed is in perplexity."

Scott would have given a less distorted picture of his country's history if he had applied himself to discovering to what an extent progress during the thirteenth century depended on the civilizing work of the Church, and how completely Alexander III identified himself with that work. " All the days of the life of this king," [1] says Fordun, " the Church of Christ flourished, her priests were duly honoured, vice was withered up, wrong came to an end, and righteousness reigned."

Without idealizing that thirteenth century too romantically we are surely justified in believing it to have been the greatest age in Scottish history and in accounting for that greatness by the explanation that the young and vigorous country was in accord not merely with the general temper of Europe but with the particular temper of its own constituent qualities. We see in this century the various parts moving steadily forward to fusion in a well-balanced whole, and assuredly far from the least among the influences for

[1] *Gesta Annalia*, lxvii. Quoted by Bellesheim.

unity was the Catholic Church. It was the Church which amalgamated Gaels, Saxons, the mysterious Picts, the Britons of Strathclyde, Normans, Flemings, Norsemen, and the rest into Scotland, and it was to be the Church which would harden the still imperfectly set amalgam to resist the heat of English aggression, when Edward, the prototype of all that has been best and all that has been worst in England through the centuries, shattered by his cunning statesmanship the peace of a hundred years and claimed a fine constructive morality for his destructive action.

When the King of England had seemingly reduced the country to a province and carried off to Westminster the Stone of Destiny a Scots mission reached Boniface VIII in Rome, pleading for his intervention. The Pope sent a letter to Edward, entrusted to the Archbishop of Canterbury, in which he pointed out that the feudal superiority over Scotland had always belonged to the Holy See, that the wardship of the Maid of Norway had not been granted to the King of England, but to a representative body of Scottish nobles, that the independence of Scotland had been guaranteed by the Treaty of Brigham, and that whatever homage had been offered by a disunited nobility to the detriment of Scottish rights and liberties should not be held binding.

How the King of England managed to persuade the

Pope that the Scots were in the wrong is not clear, but, years before, Boniface had accompanied Cardinal Ottoboni to England when the latter was sent to the help of Henry III against his rebellious barons and bishops, and he had been rescued from the Tower of London by the future Edward I. In 1302 Boniface VIII wrote letters to the bishops of Scotland calling upon them to give up all opposition to Edward and threatening penalties in the event of their refusal.

The leader of the patriotic ecclesiastics was Robert Wishart, Bishop of Glasgow, and it is certain that without him neither Wallace and Andrew of Moray at first nor Bruce himself later could have hampered and harried the English plans so successfully. If Scotland was the first country in mediaeval Europe to base its resistance to a feudal claim on its national status, the inspiration was the Scottish Church; and Edward had shown his recognition of the obstacle that Church was to his schemes by a persistent endeavour to obtrude English priests into Scottish benefices. The war against him was a holy war preached by the Scottish Church as a crusade, and when on March 27th, 1306, Bruce was defiantly crowned at Scone it was the presence of the Bishop of St Andrews, the Bishop of Glasgow, and the Bishop of Moray more than that of the few nobles and knights of Bruce's party which made that coronation anything except a shadowy ceremony. And the answer to it was excommunication by the Papal Legate in England. Edward had certainly managed to prejudice the Apostolic See against the Scottish case to some purpose. Nevertheless, not excommunication nor interdict could stop that holy war of independence.

Bannockburn was fought and won, and let it be remembered that it was fought by Catholics confident of Divine aid. The Bishop of Dunblane said Mass that famous June morning on a knoll in front of the Scottish Army and urged the soldiers to a stern defence of their country. Then in the words of the chronicler, " when the two armies approached very near each other all the Scots fell on their knees to repeat the Paternoster, commending themselves to God and seeking help from Heaven, after which they advanced boldly against the English." [1]

It was the turn of an English king to appeal to the Pope when the Scots carried the war across the border. In 1317 two cardinals reached England charged by Pope John XXII with the restoration of peace between Scotland and England. The Papal letters did not give Bruce his kingly title, and he refused to treat with the representatives of the nuncios alleging that their failure to acknowledge his regal dignity implied the

[1] Lanercost. Quoted by E. M. Barron in *The Scottish War of Independence.*

prejudgment of the question at issue. The nuncios excommunicated Bruce and his followers, a sentence which was confirmed by the Pope in a Bull dated June 13, 1320. Meanwhile, Bruce had summoned a Parliament at Arbroath and from there was addressed to the Pope that immortal letter the equal of which as an expression of the loftiest ideal of patriotism had not been heard since the *Persae* of Æschylus :

" We enjoyed peace and liberty, with the protection of the Papal See, until Edward, the late King of England, in the guise of a friend and ally, invaded and oppressed our nation, at that time without a head, unpractised in war, and suspecting no evil. The wrongs which we suffered under the tyranny of Edward are beyond description, and, indeed, they would appear incredible to all but those who actually felt them. He wasted our country, imprisoned our prelates, burnt our religious places, spoiled our ecclesiastics, and slew our people, without discrimination of age, sex, or rank. Through favour of Him who woundeth and maketh whole, we have been freed from so great and unbearable calamities by the valour of our lord and king, Robert. He, like another Joshua or Judas Maccabeus, gladly endured toils, distresses, the extremity of want, and every peril, to rescue his people and inheritance out of the hands of the enemy. Divine Providence, that legal succession which we will constantly maintain, and our due and unanimous consent, have made him our Chief and King. To him, in defence of our liberty, we are bound to adhere, as well of right as by reason of his deserts; and to him we will in all things adhere, for through him salvation has been wrought to all our people. But should he abandon our cause, or aim at reducing us or our kingdom under the domination of the English, we will instantly try to expel him as a common enemy, the subverter of our rights and his own, and we will choose another king to rule and protect us; for while a hundred of us exist we will never submit to England. We fight not for glory, wealth, or honour, but for that liberty without which no virtuous man can live."

Note that of the five complaints of Edward's tyranny three refer to his treatment of the Church, and no juster appreciation of the Papal claims and Papal duties has been given than in the concluding words of this letter :

" Wherefore, we most earnestly beseech your Holiness, that you behold with a fatherly eye the tribulations and distresses brought upon us by the English, and that you admonish Edward to content himself with his own dominions, esteemed in former times enough for seven kings, and allow us Scotsmen, who dwell in a poor and remote corner, and who seek for nought but her own, to remain in peace. In order to secure that peace we are ready to do anything that is consistent with our national interests. Should you, however, give too credulous an ear to the reports of our enemies, distrust the sincerity of our professions, and persist in favouring the English to our destruction, then we hold you guilty, in the sight of the Most High, of the loss of lives, the perdition of souls, and all the other miserable consequences which may ensue from war between the two contending nations. Ever ready, like dutiful children, to yield all fit obedience to you as God's Viceregent, we commit our cause to the Supreme King and Judge; we cast our cares on Him, and we steadily trust that He will inspire us with valour and bring our enemies to nought."

The immediate result of this appeal was that the Pope explained why he had withheld recognition of Bruce's kingship. This was followed by a suspension of the excommunication and an admonition to make peace with England.

By the Treaty of Northampton in 1328 the complete independence of Scotland and Bruce's kingship were acknowledged by Edward II, and exactly nine years to a day after the Pope had confirmed the excommunication by his legates he issued a Bull decreeing that the kings of Scotland should henceforth be anointed as well as crowned by the bishops of St

Andrews, or in default of them, by the bishops of Glasgow.

It might appear that the Scottish Church had emerged stronger and more secure from the struggles of these momentous years. So far as outward dignity was enhanced that is true; but violence must always be paid for, and when bishops had to fight like barons and priests like men-at-arms spiritual life inevitably suffered. Moreover, the patriotic prelates whose fervour had been such an inspiration of the national resistance were absent from their sees for many years. Bishop Lamberton of St Andrews and the Abbot of Scone were captured and sent to England in chains. Bishop Wishart of Glasgow, who absolved Bruce for the murder of the Red Comyn and crowned him at Scone, was a prisoner in England until after Bannockburn, and it must be held significant that the Pope, in spite of Edward's demand, refused to deprive him of his see. We get in some synodal statutes of St Andrews a hint of the martial state of the clergy during the fourteenth century when we read that priests are forbidden to wear the long knives called hangers except when equipped for a journey. From these same statutes we may gather that the old evil of clerical concubinage was still flourishing. The impression left by what we know of ecclesiastical history in Scotland during the years that succeeded the struggle for independence is that the Church was as profoundly exhausted as the nation. And throughout those years the hostility of England was persistent and relentless.

When King Robert III died in 1406, the heir to the throne, his second son James, Earl of Carrick, was a prisoner in England. He was proclaimed King at Perth, and his uncle Robert, Duke of Albany, was nominated as Regent. To help and hasten the return of King James I an embassy was despatched to France to renew the old alliance, and from that date until the accord was broken by the Reformers in their lust to impose on Scotland their revolutionary ideas with the help of England the two nations were closely linked in European politics.

The political and cultural benefits of this alliance were immense for the smaller and poorer country, but it had one disastrous spiritual result by leading Scotland into acknowledging the anti-Popes whose pretensions were supported by France in pursuit of an ambitious imperialism. And even when all Europe had acknowledged the rightful Pope the Scots for a while continued to deny him, merely to demonstrate their hatred of England.

When, in 1424, James I at last sat upon his own throne he found the Church of Scotland in as bad a state as the rest of his heritage. The energetic King lost no time in asserting his authority. Throughout his all too brief rule he made every effort to purify ecclesiastical life, and by such a purification to strengthen its ability to dam the rising flood of religious revolution. Unfortunately for his country and for the Church he was murdered in his prime through one of those conspiracies of ambitious nobles whose blind insensate egoism in century after century has been the particular curse of Scotland.

James had had an example from his captor Henry V of severity with the Lollards, and he had not been back in Scotland a year before he was securing from Parliament a direction for every bishop to search out his diocese for the existence of heretics, to punish them by the Church's laws, and if necessary to invoke the aid of the secular arm, to whose authority their anarchical social theories were considered dangerous.

During the Regency, in 1407, John Resby, an English priest, who had been working secretly with others for the spread of Wycliffite doctrines, had been burnt at Perth; but it was not until 1433 that another heretic, Paul Crawar, an emissary from the Hussites of Bohemia, was burnt at St Andrews. The persecution of Lollards in Scotland was never severe; but it is an assumption incapable of justification by the evidence of facts that the reason for this may be sought in a natural predisposition of the Scottish people to Lollard ideas. The problem for King and people alike was the aggressiveness of an unruly nobility. The loyalty of the five Jameses to the Church kept the people loyal, for the King was the defender of the commonalty. In the minority of James III it was the great and good James Kennedy, Bishop of St Andrews and Chancellor of the realm, who kept that realm together, striving for reform in every direction, ecclesiastical and secular. " In him," writes a Protestant historian,[1] " the country lost the only statesman who possessed sufficient firmness, ability, and integrity to direct the councils of government. He was indeed, in every respect, a remarkable man; a pious and conscientious churchman, munificent, active, and discriminating in his charity; and whose religion, untinged with bigotry or superstition, was pure and practical. His zeal for the interests of literature and science was another prominent and admirable feature in his character, of which he left a noble monument in St Salvator's College at St Andrews, founded by him in 1456, and richly endowed out of ecclesiastical revenues. . . . Although in his public works, in his endowments of churches, and in everything connected with the pomp and ceremonial of the Catholic faith, he was unusually magnificent, yet in his own person, and the expenditure of his private household, he exhibited a rare union of purity, decorum, and

[1] Tytler : *History of Scotland*, Vol. II, p. 196.

frugality; nor could the sternest judges breathe a single aspersion against either his integrity as a minister of State, or his private character as a minister of religion."

Yet notwithstanding the personality of Bishop Kennedy the behaviour of the nobles during the reign of James III weakened the fervour of the Church for good and fatally hindered reform when reform was urgently needed. Cathedrals and monastic chapters were deprived of their rights of election in the interests of greedy nobles, who were thus enabled to force unworthy men into important offices. The system of commendatory abbots was revived, and laymen, sometimes of tender years, held high ecclesiastical dignities to the scandal of religion. The Crown secured the fatal right to present to benefices during the vacancy of an episcopal see. And it must be remembered that these claims by the Crown to prerogatives that impugned canonical rights were forced upon it in the necessity to turn anywhere for means to strengthen itself against the continuous disloyalty and self-aggrandizement of the nobles.

Bishop Kennedy died in 1466 at a time when his influence for good was at its height and when the country was, as indeed it usually was, in a state of distraction, on this occasion caused by the feuds following upon the Treaty of Ardtornish between

Edward IV and the Lord of the Isles, by the terms of which Scotland was to be partitioned between the Earl of Douglas and the Lord of the Isles, who were to do homage to the King of England as his vassals. Kennedy was succeeded by his half-brother Patrick Graham, Bishop of Brechin. His nomination proved obnoxious to one of the noble factions; but Graham travelled to Rome and secured from Pope Paul II the confirmation of his translation. Threats of violence from home kept the new Bishop of St Andrews from returning for some time to his see, and meanwhile George Neville, Archbishop of York, revived the old claim of supremacy and jurisdiction over the Scottish Church. Graham defended the independence of the national Church so well that in 1472 Sixtus IV raised the see of St Andrews to an archbishopric and created it metropolitan church for the whole of Scotland. Galloway was removed from the five-hundred-year-old jurisdiction of York, the sees of Orkney and the Isles from the jurisdiction of Drontheim in Norway. The Archbishop of York, who was in prison at the time on a charge of high treason, protested against being deprived of a suffragan; but the Pope replied that an enemy ought not to have metropolitan rights in Scotland. Although the Norwegian Archbishop of Drontheim accepted the loss of jurisdiction over the Hebrides without protest, the argument about

Orkney continued for another fifty years and more, which was not surprising, as Orkney and Shetland had become a part of Scotland only four years previously when James III married Margaret of Denmark, for the payment of whose dowry they were the pledge.

The real opposition, however, to the new dignity accorded to St Andrews came, as alas, might have been expected, from within Scotland itself, particularly from the Bishop of Glasgow and his brother prelates. The new Archbishop had been made Apostolic Nuncio besides and as such was called upon to tax a tenth of benefices in all dioceses for a crusade against the Turk. Astonishing charges were brought against Archbishop Graham, so astonishing as to warrant the presumption that the Archbishop's mind had given way. In 1478 after a long investigation he was found guilty and sentenced to be deprived of his dignities, degraded from his orders, and imprisoned for life in a monastery. He died in the year of his condemnation, and was succeeded by William Sheves, who was Archdeacon of St Andrews and one of the chief witnesses against him.

The whole melancholy business is wrapped in obscurity, but the Bull of deprivation refers to the testimony of the King, the clergy and people, and the Chapter and University of St Andrews, so that we are bound to accept the decision of the Holy See as just. The whole case must have had a most injurious effect on the Scottish Church, which at that critical period could ill stand the repercussions of such a scandal.

The new Archbishop devoted himself to strengthening his ecclesiastical position, and in 1487 a Bull of Innocent VIII conferred on him the same privileges as the Archbishop of Canterbury, with the dignity of Primate of all Scotland and *legatus natus*. This again roused the jealousy of Glasgow, which with the support of Parliament protested against the new pre-eminence of St Andrews. Innocent VIII granted to the Bishop of Glasgow exemption from the jurisdiction of the Primate during his lifetime. This did not satisfy Glasgow. In 1489 a resolution was passed by Parliament, demanding the erection of Glasgow into an archbishopric with the same privileges as York, and King James IV, who was a canon of Glasgow, wrote urgently to the Pope in advocacy of the step. In 1492 Innocent VIII gave way and raised Glasgow to an archbishopric, with Dunkeld, Dunblane, Galloway, and Argyll for suffragan sees. He refused the *pallium*, however, and also the dignity of Primate and *legatus natus*; but he granted to Glasgow and its suffragan sees exemption from the primatial and legatine authority of St Andrews during the lives of their present occupants.   This compromise satisfied neither Archbishop, and the unseemly contest was prolonged until Parliament enacted that the rival prelates were to abide by the judgment of the Holy See on pain of having their revenues confiscated.   James IV tried to have the Archbishop of Glasgow created a Cardinal; but the Pope refused.

On the death of Archbishop Sheves in 1497 the King's brother, the Duke of Ross, aged twenty-one, was elected to the primatial see; but it is not certain that he was consecrated before his death in 1503.   The next nomination was even less suitable, for Alexander Stuart, a natural son of the King by Mary Boyd, was only sixteen at the death of the Duke of Ross, and the see was kept vacant for him six years until his own education was completed.   He returned from his studies at Padua and Sienna as Archbishop-elect in 1509.   Two years later he was made Chancellor, appointed legate *a latere* by Pope Julius II, and given the Abbey of Dunfermline and the priory of Coldingham *in commendam*.   James IV now transferred his support of the see of Glasgow to St Andrews, and when Archbishop Blackadder of Glasgow died on pilgrimage in Palestine the King asked the Pope not to renew the exemption from the Primacy of St Andrews.   In 1513 the young Archbishop fell fighting beside his father at Flodden, being then but twenty-six years of age.

Flodden! Sir Walter Scott is somewhat unctuously sure that the alleged appearance of Saint John to the King in the church of Linlithgow and the Apostle's warning of him in the presence of his assembled courtiers against the proposed invasion of England is only one more "Roman Catholic" imposture. It may be so. Nevertheless, when we reflect on the immediate and ultimate woes that battle of Flodden brought to Scotland, the least superstitious Scotsman might be justified in believing that Almighty God had of His mercy granted this warning to a nation before it plunged downward to political, moral, and spiritual ruin. The irony of it is that James IV was right in his proposed line of action from the point of view both of honour and expediency. When Henry VIII invaded France it was Scotland's opportunity to make an effective entry upon the European scene. A victorious invasion of England would have changed the international situation, and if the battle of Flodden had been fought with as much tactical skill as gallantry it would have been won. The most superficial speculation upon the result of such a victory at this critical moment in history will suggest an almost infinite vista of possibilities. But Flodden was lost. James was killed. The widow of that calamitous Tudor marriage, the avaricious wanton Margaret, evil sister of an evil brother, lived on.

Scotland with her baby King receded from the European scene to become again the prey of noble factions in that obscure twilight from which James IV had brought her into the glittering morning tide of the Renaissance.

It may seem astonishing that the storm of religious revolution did not break over Scotland long before it did. The Church there suffered no less than the Church everywhere else from abuses of which the disorder of the times prevented reformation until it was too late to stem the onset of Protestantism. While the very foundations of the Catholic Church quivered, Glasgow and St Andrews were back at their quarrels over primatial jurisdiction.

The fact is that the new religious ideas making headway all over Europe were making very little headway in Scotland. The persecution of Lollards had been slight, and when in 1494 some thirty people had been summoned before the Archbishop of Glasgow to answer before the King for their heresies they were sent off with nothing more severe than a warning to beware of new doctrines. We hear no more of heresy until 1525 when Parliament passed an Act forbidding the importation of Lutheran books and the dissemination of Lutheran opinions.

After the death of the young Archbishop of St Andrews at Flodden it was proposed to translate to the vacant see the saintly Bishop Elphinstone from Aberdeen. That great prelate, stricken by the news of Flodden, from which he never recovered, declined the primacy, and there was a contest between three candidates which was finally resolved by the nomination of Andrew Foreman, Bishop of Moray, by Pope Leo X. The new Archbishop, who was able and energetic, made a strenuous effort during his short episcopate to put ecclesiastical matters in order. The statutes of a diocesan synod held during his primacy are evidence of a determination to reform the Church in spite of the wild anarchy in the country during the minority of James V. These statutes aim at improving the moral and material condition of the clergy, at enhancing the solemnity of divine worship, and at promoting learning. The three universities of St Andrews, Glasgow, and Aberdeen had all owed their foundation to the Church, and the welfare of these universities depended entirely on that Church. However, it is idle to waste words in discussing individual exceptions to the degeneracy into which the Church had sunk after human frailty had thwarted the sublime hopes of the Middle Ages. The time had come for the purgation of that Church to be secured by the effort to resist the gates of Hell, the time when for a while there seemed nothing for faith to cling to except the promise of Christ that those gates should not prevail against His Church. And in no country might despair have seemed more utterly justified than in Scotland, for against no country were the gates of Hell unlocked by a merciful God with such apparent mercilessness.

Few Scotsmen with any pretensions to historical knowledge are found nowadays to defend the means by which the Reformation was forced upon their country. They recognize that the motives of the chief actors were greed and ambition, the methods violence and treachery, the deciding factors English money and English pikes. Most of them, however, console themselves with the fancy that the Reformation was an expression of Divine truth and therefore ultimately an expression of good. Others, rejecting the Christian revelation, deplore the crimes of the Reformers against beauty and decency, but remain undisturbed by its crimes against truth and morals. A minority, but thanks be to God, an ever-increasing minority, recognizes that the wrongness of the means was equalled only by the wrongness of the end. Those people understand why the average Scotsman regards the Irishman with aversion and why the average Irishman regards the Scotsman with contempt.

CHAPTER III

THE earliest really serious threat to the stability of the Catholic Church in Scotland came from the propagation of Lutheran opinions, and after the Act of 1525 already mentioned proceedings under it were taken against the first Scotsman to be arraigned for heresy. This was Patrick Hamilton, a young man in his mid-twenties, who was connected both with the Royal family and the house of Arran, and who, according to the pernicious custom of the time, was lay commendator of the Abbey of Fearn. He had studied abroad and come into personal contact with Luther and Melancthon. Returning to Scotland in 1527, after having been advised to leave the country, he seems to have disseminated Protestant ideas partly from sincere conviction and partly as a way of striking at the Douglas faction which was maintaining its power by holding the King in custody. Hamilton was given a second chance to leave the country; but, trusting to his friends, he stood his ground. He was arrested and on being found guilty of heresy was handed over to the secular arm to be dealt with according to the law. The execution was hastened in expectation of a rescue, and on February 29th, 1528, the sentence was carried out at St Andrews. Hamilton met death with fortitude, and his confident demeanour undoubtedly gave a new prestige to the doctrines with which he had identified himself. " The reek of Patrick Hamilton," it was said, " infected all it blew on." A dozen or so promoters of the subversive doctrines, unhappy apostate friars and priests mostly, were burnt during the next decade, and in 1535 Parliament passed another Act against Lutheran propaganda.

It was in 1535, too, that Henry VIII invited his young nephew James V to visit him at York to negotiate a marriage with the Princess Mary and to discuss the future of the Reformation. Henry had proclaimed himself supreme head of the Church of England in the previous year, and he was now anxious to break up the alliance between France and Scotland in order to further his own schemes for the national dignity and political aggrandizement of England. To provide a spiritual background for these schemes Henry was evolving that national church which was to be given enduring shape by his daughter Elizabeth. The meeting at York was postponed, and an embassy was sent from Scotland to France instead, to negotiate a royal marriage there. Henry VIII liked the look of affairs less and less when the Scottish King was wedded to the only daughter of the King of France. He started to make things difficult for James by helping the intrigues of the Douglases and of his own sister Margaret, the queen-mother. Of all the misfortunes that afflicted the House of Stuart that black Tudor blood mingling with theirs was perhaps the worst. Henry made little headway at first. James on his return from France had behind him the support of the clergy, the love of the commons, and the loyalty of a sufficient number of nobles. He intended to act in close co-operation with the French King and the Emperor. He was high in favour with the Pope. The eyes of Europe were upon him, and upon his realm of Scotland.

Queen Magdalen lived only a few weeks after she left Scotland. In the following year James married Mary of Guise, and the close relations with France were not interrupted. The statesman behind James was David Beaton, a great ecclesiastic and a great patriot, whose vigour and ability thwarted the plans of the English king to include Scotland in his new Imperium, of which he was to be the Divine Augustus. In December, 1538, Beaton was created Cardinal, and a month later he succeeded his uncle as Archbishop of St Andrews. Henry tried to upset his influence with James by sending him certain letters from Beaton to the Pope of which he had obtained possession and which, judging James by himself, he hoped would rouse his suspicious jealousy. It was no use. James held to the Cardinal. He had no intention of plundering the Church as his uncle was suggesting he should, because it was the Church's financial and moral support which enabled him to contend with a horde of self-seeking nobles. Henry who had proclaimed himself King of Ireland was disturbed by the news that the Irish Chiefs had sent a mission to Scotland, offering the crown to James. On top of that he was enraged to hear that Pope Paul III had conferred on James his own pet title of Defender of the Faith bestowed on him by Paul III's predecessor, Leo X, in gratitude for his defence of the Catholic doctrine of the Sacraments against Luther. Henry's vanity stung him into a formal protest: he had a high opinion of his own theology. Diplomacy having failed, the English King had recourse to open war, victory in which he had secured beforehand by intrigue. If the King of Scotland would not " reform " the Scottish Church for the sake of what he could make out of the transaction, the King of Scotland's esurient nobles were tempted by the rich prospect, and they yielded to it. On the shameful field of Solway Moss three thousand Scotsmen led by such nobles bolted before three hundred English troopers. The leaders allowed themselves to be made prisoners, afterwards buying their liberty by a vow to enslave their country. James when he heard of the disgraceful rout was seized by a fever and shut himself up in the palace of Falkland. Here they brought him the news of his daughter's birth. " God's will be done. It came with a lass, and it will go with a lass," said the stricken king, contemplating the beginning and the end of his House as rulers of Scotland. Then he turned his face to the wall, and six days later he died of a broken heart in the thirty-second year of his age.

Beside that infant Queen's cradle-throne there stood, almost alone in loyalty and patriotic determination, Cardinal Beaton. He was the rustless spearhead of Scotland's resistance to Henry's aggression. The Regent Arran began to encourage the Reformed doctrines, and the English faction managed to get the Cardinal imprisoned. Henry had bribed with pensions a number of Scottish nobles to sign a covenant in which they acknowledged him as lord paramount of Scotland, pledged themselves to put into his hands all the Scottish strongholds, and entrust the infant Queen to his guardianship.[1] If Parliament refused to ratify this covenant, these hireling nobles were to help Henry conquer the country by force of arms. A Parliament consisting largely of these Anglicizing

[1] The obese Henry was striding toward his goal with the long shanks of Edward I.

nobles agreed to the principle of the future marriage of the infant Queen with the Prince of Wales, but lacked the impudence to accept the rest of the arrangement.

Scotland had been laid under an interdict after the imprisonment of the Cardinal, and it does not suggest that the Reformed doctrines had made as much progress as is claimed, except among a nobility hungry for the Church's wealth, when we find that it was the people's wrath at their deprivation of the Sacraments which compelled the release of the Cardinal.

Beaton immediately summoned a general convention of the bishops and clergy at St Andrews, and by a tax on benefices raised the sum of ten thousand pounds toward a war in defence of national independence. The clergy resolved to give all their money, to melt down their own plate and the Church's plate, and even to fight in person if it was necessary. Beaton's enthusiasm had roused the country to a patriotic fervour, the like of which had not been known for two hundred and fifty years. Arran himself with trembling lips abjured his errors in the Franciscan Church at Stirling. He had been bought by Henry with the half-promise of the hand of Elizabeth and the throne of Scotland as her father's vassal. This infamous bargain he now repudiated. The nobles in English pay, to escape impeachment for high treason, bound themselves " to remain true, faithful, and obedient servants to their sovereign lady and her authority, to assist the lord governor for defence of the realm against their old enemies of England, to support the liberties of Holy Church, and to maintain the true Christian faith."

So much for their religious sincerity.

Henry VIII, who saw that his ambitious plans could never materialize as long as Beaton was alive, now entered into a plot to have the Cardinal assassinated, one of the go-betweens in which was George Wishart. This man, under the protection of the Protestant nobles and lairds, who were working up mob violence with the help of demagogues like Wishart in the hope of future plunder, had been preaching round about the country for two years. The Cardinal, learning of the plot to assassinate him and of Wishart's share in it, gave orders for his apprehension; but the preacher surrounded himself with an armed guard, and it was not until January, 1546, that the Earl of Bothwell achieved the arrest. In the charges against Wishart we find that he had gone beyond the Lollards and the Lutherans by denying the Real Presence in the Eucharist. This denial was logically inevitable from men concerned to deny the priestly office. The right of private judgment carried with it as a corollary the validity of private action. Wishart was found guilty and handed over to the secular arm for execution. There can be no doubt the condemned man's bold demeanour was considerably helped by his belief that the plot to murder the Cardinal would anticipate his own violent end. The supposed prophecy of his enemy's doom, which has been accorded a Divine inspiration by many credulous Protestants, was actually inspired by the secret information of an accessory before the fact; but it was not until on May 29, 1546, that four assassins gained admission to the Castle of St Andrews and cut down the great Cardinal with their swords.

David Beaton has been accused of ruthless cruelty. The answer to that charge is the small number of persons who suffered death under his administration—seven in all. None of these was tortured, and even his personal enemy Wishart suffered less on the scaffold than the Jacobite martyrs of Kennington and Carlisle, being strangled on the scaffold before the flames touched his dead body. David Beaton has been accused of bigotry. The answer to that charge is the compulsion of the truth. If his faith was sincere, and his worst foes do not accuse him of insincerity, bigotry was demanded by the ruinous subversion of that faith by those who he could not but believe were emissaries of Satan. David Beaton has been accused of poisoning James V, of forging his will, of an amour with the Queen-Mother, and of a generally libertine existence. These charges were never made in his lifetime, and they rest on the bare assertions of his avowed enemies without a shred of evidence to support them. It should have been remembered by the Protestant historians who gave them common currency that charges of an even graver kind supported by much more credible testimony were levelled against John Knox.

David Beaton stands with Bruce and Wallace, with Andrew of Moray and that earlier and nobler Wishart of Glasgow, among the great patriots of a country which has produced an unenviable number of traitors. The doom of the hapless four-year-old Queen of Scots was sealed when on that fatal dawn of May the Cardinal in the forty-fifth year of his age sank beneath the sword of the elder Leslie, with the Master of Rothes and James Melville and Kirkcaldy of Grange standing by. The conspirators notified the English King of the useful deed and begged his help to defend the Castle of St Andrews where they had been joined by various supporters of the English party. Henry VIII sent them £1180, and communication with England was for a while maintained by sea.

Among those who joined the band in St Andrews was John Knox. Little is known of this man's career before he joined the sinister collection of drunkards, debauchees, and religious maniacs in that castle, the ruins of which even to this day chill the imaginative mind with a sense of past evil. He was almost certainly in minor orders, but that he was never a priest the Catholic has good reason to hope. His own occupation at St Andrews was tutoring the sons of lairds and discoursing on the Scriptures. We have Buchanan's[1] testimony that the band of rebels terrorized the countryside with fire and sword and indulged in every kind of debauchery. An apostate friar, John Rough, called Knox to the public ministry, and in his acceptation of office of preacher from that disorderly band of murderers, rebels, and traitors to Scotland we may find the first authentic manifestation of Presbyterianism. Just over a year after the murder of Cardinal Beaton French galleys summoned to his aid by Arran appeared off the castle and a week later the conspirators surrendered and were taken away to France as prisoners. Knox was kept in one of the galleys until he was released in February 1549 through the intercession of Edward VI of England, in whose realm he found security and self-importance.

Henry VIII had died in 1547; but the Protector Somerset, secure of the active help of over two hundred Scottish nobles, whose names and Judas-fees were discovered in the Castle of St Andrews after its

[1] *Rerum Scoticarium Historia.*

surrender, invaded Scotland with a force of 18,000 men.

On September 10th, 1547, the Scottish army of defence under the Regent Arran was bloodily defeated at Pinkie Cleugh near Musselburgh. Treachery seems to have been the determining factor. In the ranks of the Scottish army were many of the clergy unarmed but determined to take the field in fulfilment of their patriotic vow. They marched under a white banner, whose device was a woman weeping at the foot of a crucifix with the legend *Afflictae sponsae ne obliviscaris.* " Forget not thy stricken bride." Many of these devoted priests were slain, and the white banner was trampled beneath the feet of the enemy. September 9th, 1513: Flodden. September 10th, 1547: Pinkie.

The Queen-Mother acted with resolution to repel the English invasion. She proposed a marriage between Mary and the Dauphin of France and her removal to the French Court to be educated. The French landed troops at Leith. The little Queen left Dunbarton, and after a stormy voyage reached France safely, evading the English fleet on the way. The Scots and French pressed the English hard, driving them out of one stronghold after another. Finally the English sued for peace, which was proclaimed in April, 1550. Four years later Arran resigned from the Regency which was assumed by Mary of Guise, the

Queen-Mother, a wise and tolerant woman with the interests of her adopted country at heart. Edward VI had died and had been succeeded by Mary, which made the Queen-Mother's task easier for a while, until the accession of Elizabeth brought about a return of English aggression. On the other hand the flight from England to Scotland of Protestant preachers gave fresh vitality to subversive propaganda, and the reformation of the Scottish Church from within which had been proceeding steadily was much hampered. The extraordinary restraint of the Catholics suggests the lethargy of self-confidence arising from a complete failure to appreciate the seriousness of the outlook, and it may offer an explanation for the feebleness of their resistance to the storm that was to burst over them a few years later. From the murder of Beaton until the arrival of the Protestant preachers from over the border there was only one execution for heresy.

In spite of that toleration, John Knox, when he fled from England to escape the penalty for preaching heresy there, thought it prudent to avoid his native country, and betook himself instead to Geneva. In estimating the character of Knox this unfortunate cowardice must always be kept in mind, for the man himself was acutely aware of it, as we may gather from his letters. Indeed, it was his own consciousness of such cowardice that preyed upon an already warped and soured imagination, and drove him to take refuge from it in the bluster under which he strove to conceal what in the fashionable jargon we call an inferiority complex. It was thoroughly successful with his contemporaries, who accepted Knox's valuation of himself as the true one. Some of his excessive religious arrogance may have been due to an uneasy doubt at the back of his mind about his ultimate salvation, for he was under the perpetual necessity of reassuring himself that the denial of Jesus Christ in the Blessed Sacrament was not a blasphemy by denying Him more emphatically. That there was something wrong with the man is clear enough, but we are not entitled on the facts at our disposal to assert that he was utterly bad. We must make allowances for the effect of that brutally coarse nature upon the imagination of his enemies, when we hear of a sexual life that exposed him to the suspicions of the scandalous. For instance, that friendship with Elizabeth Bowes, the wife of a man of family in the north of England, does not demand an unpleasant interpretation. This melancholic female whose mind was continuously depressed by religious gloom had promised him the hand of her fifth daughter Marjory. Marjory's father strongly objected, and in the end Mrs Bowes joined John Knox and her daughter in Geneva. The letters between the preacher and his disciple, a woman of his own age, in

57

which he signs himself " your Son " provide an interesting if repulsive study in morbid religiosity. It is noteworthy that in one of these letters Knox actually expresses a doubt of his being one of the elect, and this private dread of damnation should be remembered when we hear of his confident ravings in the pulpit.

Knox found his spiritual home in Geneva, and it became his heart's desire to establish in Scotland a comparable theocracy. In 1554 the Scottish Reformer received a call to be one of the pastors of the English congregation at Frankfurt-on-the-Main, a call which he accepted willingly " at the commandment of that notable servant of God, John Calvin," who had just had the wretched Servetus burnt alive for doctrinal eccentricity. The usual domestic quarrels of Presbyterianism broke out. Dr Richard Cox came over with some Protestant exiles from England, and presently the small congregation was split into " Coxians " and " Knoxians," the new-comers insisting on making responses after the minister in spite of admonitions by Knox and the senior members. Thus early are foreshadowed what the old Highlander, quoted in the first chapter, called the splinters of a church. The quarrel ended in Knox's receiving an order from the magistrates to quit Frankfurt, which he did after preaching a sermon at his lodgings on the Resurrection and the joys being got ready for the elect. Did these include the contemplation of his eternally damned opponents?

After a brief sojourn again at Geneva, Knox heard such favourable accounts of the toleration of the Regent Queen-Mother that he felt it was safe for him to return to Scotland. He was not molested for some time, and assisted by the protection of Protestant nobles and lairds he declared loudly and ubiquitously his hatred of the Catholic Church and above all of the idolatrous Mass. At last he was summoned to appear before the ecclesiastical authorities at the Blackfriars' Church in Edinburgh. Knox arrived like a feudal lord with a levy of armed retainers, and probably in fear of a clash of arms the Bishops quashed the proceedings. Knox emboldened by this hint of pusillanimity preached openly in Edinburgh " in a greater audience than ever before he had done in that town." [1] Nevertheless he was not inclined to try his immunity too hardly, and a few weeks after this, having received a call to the pastoral care of the English Protestants in Geneva, he left Scotland again. What made John Knox shrink from a glorious martyrdom? We might reply that the fervour of a faith which is inspired by denying the faith of others does not warm the mind to face death; but stark fright provides a simpler and more intelligible answer. He was tried in his absence,

[1] Knox : *Historie of the Reformation.*

found guilty, and burnt in effigy. From the security of Geneva he published, *The Appellation of John Knox from the cruell and most unjust Sentence pronounced against him by the false bishops and clergie of Scotland; with his Supplication and Exhortation to the Nobility, States, and Commonalty of the same Realme.* In this work a notable servant of God pleads the duty of every individual member of the commonwealth to murder all those guilty of idolatry, that is all those who believe that the Son of God is present upon His altar in the Sacred Host.

In the Spring of 1557 some of the Protestant Scottish lords wrote begging Knox to come home, all being safe again. On reaching Dieppe in the autumn the preacher received some discouraging communications and promptly turned back to Geneva, where he had the moral temerity to write a letter upbraiding his supporters for their own cowardice and urging them to make a move even at the risk of their lives.

The Protestant lords met on December 3rd, 1557, and subscribed the Solemn League and Covenant, binding themselves to maintain the Congregation (the name for themselves and their party) and to " forsake and renounce the congregation of Satan, with all the superstition and idolatry thereof." The apostasy from the Catholic Church thus formally subscribed is signed at the head by the Earl of Argyll, who had sold himself to England for a thousand crowns. Several of the other signatories were English pensioners. The Lords of the Congregation, within the sphere of their armed influence, proceeded to eject Catholic priests and install preachers who were to read the English Book of Common Prayer. Letters were sent to Calvin, asking him to order Knox to return to Scotland. The Lords of the Congregation had waited long enough for their plunder. They wanted the demagogue whose "rash ranting" would unloose the passions of the mob and start the convenient anarchy. Yet Knox still dallied, and if it were not from cowardice from what impulse was it?

The failure of the Queen-Regent to come to grips at once with the Lords of the Congregation was due to her anxiety over the French marriage for which she desired the ratification of Parliament. She feared Arran, the late Regent, as heir-presumptive to the throne; and the possibility of a rebellion against her daughter made her anxious for the support of the Protestant lords. Now indeed was a David Beaton needed. No comparable figure appeared upon the darkening scene of the Scots tragedy.

What was to be the last Provincial Council of the Scottish Church for three hundred and twenty-six years sat at Edinburgh in March and April, 1559. It passed a series of wise reforms; but it was too late.

On May 2nd Knox, assured of a safe retreat over the border now that Elizabeth was Queen of England, landed at Leith, and reached Dundee where the Protestant lords in arms mustered round him. The Queen-Regent, at the instance of her Guise brothers, had recently joined the League to re-establish the Catholic faith in Europe, and a French embassy had arrived to discuss the measures to be taken in Scotland. A proclamation had been published to prohibit anybody from preaching or administering the sacraments without the authority of the bishops. The Protestant preachers had disregarded this and had been summoned to Stirling on the 10th of May to answer for their defiance. The Lords of the Congregation, determined to support the preachers, gathered at Perth where in St John's Church on the following day Knox thundered out one of those fierce sermons against idolatry. After the sermon a priest prepared to say Mass by opening the triptych on the altar. Some youth in the congregation, intoxicated by the preacher's eloquence, cried out against the idolatry of the action. The priest struck him, whereupon the youth flung a stone and broke one of the statues in the reredos. This drove the mob, already maddened by inflammatory words, into a phrenzy of action, and they proceeded to wreck the church. Having tasted blood, they rioted through the city, destroying the Dominican and

Franciscan convents, and even the glorious Charter-house where James I was buried. From Perth the iconoclastic fury spread to Cupar-Fife.

Modern sensitiveness over the destruction of beauti-ful edifices and ornaments has induced aesthetic Protestants to suggest that Knox tried to restrain the mob. There are no grounds for supposing he did anything but incite them. He revelled, like so many cowards, in the sense of power whenever and in whatever shape it came to him. In any case, those who believe that the end was a greater sin against God and man than the worst means taken to achieve that end must always be a little impatient of the most plausible excuses made for the means. If the end was a sin, the criminality of the means added nothing to it. The Protestant who rejoices in the destruction is at least consistent with his negative creed.

Assured of English help, the Congregation addressed a letter to the Scottish clergy which begins, " To the generation of Anti-Christ, the pestilent prelates and their shavelings within Scotland, the Congregation of Christ Jesus within the same, sayeth," and continues by warning the clergy that they would be exterminated like the Canaanites if they did not abandon their open idolatry and dealt with as murderers if they did not cease betimes from their " blinde rage."

The Queen-Regent led her forces against Perth

where the rebels had been strongly reinforced. However, Argyll and Lord James Stuart, the Queen's bastard brother, patched things up for the moment, and the Protestants evacuated Perth. Soon afterwards Argyll and Lord James, sniffing the flowing tide, went over openly to the Congregation, which was summoned to assemble at St Andrews. Knox accompanied by various Protestant nobles and their armed retainers preached at Crail and Anstruther, and the churches were subsequently wrecked by the mob. He then announced he would preach in St Andrews itself. Archbishop Hamilton tried to prevent him, but the armed Protestants were too strong. The sermon was preached. The mob turned upon the cathedral itself. Statues were overthrown. Missals, manuscripts, records, and registers were burnt. The gold and silver ornaments were pillaged. The ancient fane which had taken one hundred and sixty years to build became the bleak ruin of to-day. Monasteries, convents, and churches were now destroyed in many parts of the country. Even the abbey and palace of Scone were burnt; but of course the Stone of Destiny was safe in England under the coronation throne of Queen Elizabeth. The rebels under Argyll and Lord James marched southward, destroying on their way the churches of Stirling and Linlithgow. Finally on June 29th, the followers of the Congregation marched into Edinburgh, where every religious edifice was sacked and many of them levelled to the ground. Not yet glutted with loot, the rebels plundered the royal Treasury and seized the Mint.

At this moment Henry II of France died and was succeeded by Francis II so that Mary, Queen of Scots, was now Queen of France as well. French troops reached Scotland. An apostolic nuncio reconciled the collegiate Church of St Giles which had been desecrated by the Protestants. The Regent issued proclamations against the rebels accusing them of high treason. Although the Congregation was still sacking abbeys like Paisley and Dunfermline, its leaders were uneasy. Knox had offended Elizabeth by his denunciation of female rule in his Blast against the Monstrous Regiment of Women, but in July of 1559 he wrote a submissive letter to crave her support. Cecil was encouraging the Congregation by correspondence. Then Knox was sent to negotiate at Berwick, where he promised that the Congregation would seize Stirling and hold it if the English would pay the troops and put in a little extra for the " comfortable support " of some of the nobles.[1]

The negotiations between the hungry Lords of the Congregation and Elizabeth were protracted; but at last on February 27th, 1560, a treaty was signed at

[1] *State Papers (Scotland)*, *Eliz.*, Vol. I, No. 97.

Berwick avowedly against the political pretensions of France and without a word in it about religion.

The spiritual professions of Knox have receded conveniently into the background.

An English army, 8000 strong, invaded Scotland in April 1560, and simultaneously a fleet of fourteen ships of war anchored off Leith. The Queen-Regent's troops put up a sturdy and effective resistance for some time, but could not keep the troops of the Congregation from ravaging the country and demolishing glorious abbeys like Melrose. Mary of Guise, worn out by the efforts she had made to preserve peace, guard her daughter's throne, and serve the Church, fell sick in Edinburgh Castle. On her death-bed she sent for the Lords of Congregation and begged their loyalty for the Queen of Scots. Her last hours were tormented by the exhortations of an apostate friar called Willock, and harassed to the ultimate sigh she expired on June 10th, 1560.

The character of Mary of Guise was one of singular beauty. She had as hard a task as any woman has had to bear, and she bore it with resolution, with piety, and with extreme loving-kindness. Knox alone of historians in the filthiest language slandered her memory. His disgusting accusations are the sewage of a mind so obviously foul as to confirm a belief in those vices from the guilt of which his champions have found no contemporary evidence to exonerate him with any certitude.

A month after the death of the Queen-Regent the Treaty of Edinburgh was signed. By its provisions a Parliament was to be summoned on the following 1st of August. A council of state was to be formed immediately to take the place of the Regency. This was to consist of twelve members, seven chosen by the Queen and five by the Estates. An Act of Indemnity for the late disorders was to be passed. Armed musterings in future were to count as rebellion. Ecclesiastics whose persons or property had been injured were to receive compensation from Parliament. Religious questions were to be remitted to King Francis and Queen Mary for settlement by persons nominated in the coming Parliament.

In due course Parliament met and was packed by Protestant lairds who had no legal right to sit in it. Moreover, this Parliament assembled without the sovereign's writ and many of those present challenged its legality. In spite of these objections the Parliament voted itself to be legally in order and proceeded to business under the Speakership of Maitland of Lethington. The first item was a memorial from the Protestants, praying for the abolition of the doctrines and clergy of the Catholic Church and suggesting that the money and land which had already been seized by the nobles should be handed over to the preachers. Simultaneously Knox was thundering demands from the pulpit for all this ecclesiastical property. Parliament side-stepped the money question, but agreed that a " Confession of Faith professed and believed by the Protestants in the realm of Scotland " should be laid before the legislature. The packed assembly by a sweeping majority voted in favour of adopting it, three of the Catholic bishops and a few nobles alone voting against it. The adopting of this Confession of Faith was a violation of the clause in the Treaty of Edinburgh which provided for the remission of the religious question to the Queen and King Consort.

The Catholic bishops decided they could do nothing except enter a protest against the irregularity of the proceedings, in the evident expectation that such a Parliament would never be recognized. That was not the belief of Parliament itself, which went on to pass three more acts. The first abolished the juris-diction of the Pope. The second repealed all statutes in favour of the Catholic Church. The third made hearing or saying Mass in future punishable for the first offence by confiscation of all the offender's goods, for the second by banishment, and for the third by death.

The final act of this Parliament was to violate

another clause of the Treaty of Edinburgh by confiscating the whole property of the Church.

The Confession of Faith in 1560 was followed early in the next year by the Book of Discipline, which significantly included with the Gospel the Old Testament on which the new religion relied for Divine authority more than upon the New Testament. The holy days like Christmas and Easter were abolished, except Sunday which was to return to the primitive respectability of the Jewish Sabbath. All the edifices and foundations of the Christian faith were to be destroyed except parish churches and schools, and by a stroke of unconscious humour the dwelling-houses of the clergy with their gardens and orchards. The people were to elect their own ministers, and beyond an examination by ministers and elders no other form of ordination was to be tolerated, " for albeit the apostles used the imposition of hands, yet seeing the miracle is ceased, the using of the ceremony we judge not to be necessary." Officials called Superintendents were established, whose business was to " travel from place to place for establishing of the Church." They recall the Commissars in the early days of the Soviet forcing Communism upon the Russian nation against the desire of the majority, for, of course, the great bulk of Scotland was still Catholic in 1561. There was to be a schoolmaster in every parish and colleges in the chief towns for more advanced studies. It was vital to indoctrinate the youth of the country. The rest of the Book of Discipline was mostly taken up with various abolitions. Death was recommended as a punishment for adultery, and at the burial of the dead, adulterous or chaste, there were to be neither prayers nor singing, sermon nor ceremony.

The first General Assembly of the Reformed Church, which consisted almost entirely of laymen, met in Edinburgh on December 20th, 1560, and on December 27th, two days after the feast which celebrates the birth of the Redeemer, this Assembly was demanding " sharp punishment " for the idolaters who continued to hear Mass in Nithsdale, Galloway, Kyle, Cunningham, Carrick, Ettrick Forest, East Lothian and Fife with a special mention of the parishes of Maybole, Girvan, Kirkoswald, and Dailly " within the kirks wherof messe is openly said and maintained."

On May 27th, 1561, the second General Assembly was held, at which a petition was drawn up for Parliament, setting forth that the " Generation of Antichrist were erecting their idolatry anew," and threatening to take up the sword if penal measures were not set on foot immediately.

" Thereupon," wrote [1] Archbishop Spottiswood in 1639, " ensued a pitiful vastation of churches and

---

[1] *History of the Church and State of Scotland.*

church buildings throughout all the parts of the realm; for everyone made bold to put to their hands, the meaner sort imitating the ensample of the greater and those who were in authority. No difference was made, but all the churches were either defaced or pulled to the ground. The holy vessels, and whatsoever else men could make gain of, as timber, lead, and bells, were put to sale. The very sepulchres of the dead were not spared. The registers of the church and *bibliothèques* were cast into the fire. In a word, all was ruined, and what had escaped in the time of the first tumult did now undergo the common calamity; which was so much the worse, that the violences committed at this time were coloured with the warrant of public authority. Some ill-advised preachers did likewise animate the people in these their barbarous proceedings, crying out ' that the places where idols had been worshipped ought by the law of God to be destroyed, and that the sparing of them was the reserving of things execrable. . . .' " The report also went that John Knox (whose sayings were by many esteemed as oracles) should in one of his sermons say " that the sure way to banish the rooks was to pull down their nests. . . ."

The Reformation in Scotland was accomplished. In a similar fashion the Bolshevik revolution was imposed on Russia. Indeed, the history of Europe

since the war of 1914–18 offers repeated parallels for
the way in which the Reformation was carried through
in various countries, and after Fascism, Hitlerism,
Bolshevism, and other less successful political experi-
ments, it is much easier to understand the apparent
spontaneity with which the revolutionary religious
doctrines were welcomed.

That the Catholic clergy themselves were to a large
extent to blame for the whole business cannot be
denied. Long years of an inherited faith had made
them careless of their responsibilities, and neglectful
of their duties. Indeed it might be true to say that the
greatest sin of the Scottish clergy was their failure to
esteem that Mass of which they were at last to be
deprived by a just God, using as the instruments of
His wrath the basest of mankind. To slovenliness in
the discharge of their religious obligations could be
added in too many cases a looseness of behaviour
unworthy of the priestly dignity. Nor were the
bishops themselves always sufficiently respectful to
their own exalted office. It was meet that the penalty
should be paid. The Church needed the humiliation
Almighty God inflicted, and not the least bitter part of
that humiliation was the comparative fervour of
Protestantism at its beginning.

Yet that fury of spiritual pride which welded
the essentially individualistic creed of Protestantism

into an apparent homogeneity was bound, like any religious or political chain the strength of which is its strongest link, to depend ultimately for its endurance upon an ability to produce fanatics. The rapidity with which Protestantism all over the world and in all its myriad manifestations is now crumbling away into a negligible emotional convention, from which perhaps within less than a century it will have become a heap of inconspicuous ashes, is evidence enough by itself of the validity of that tremendous promise made to Peter by His Saviour. Comparable to that undistinguished decline of Protestantism is the equally undistinguished decline of the country which began the downward movement with such a spectacular attempt at self-destruction in the year 1560. We have noted the penalty of spiritual complacency. We have now to survey, with an ironical memory of that arrogant doctrine of predestinarianism and its logical consequences, the penalty of spiritual pride.

CHAPTER IV

Adieu, plaisant pays de France
     O ma patrie
     La plus chérie,
Qui as nourri ma jeune enfance—
Adieu, France! adieu mes beaux jours.

WITH these poignant and prophetic words Mary, Queen of Scots, returning to Scotland after the death of her youthful husband, the King of France, looked back to watch Calais vanish in that sea-fog, by the help of which, her vessel was to elude the English ships-of-war, despatched by the anxious Elizabeth to capture a beautiful rival, and bring her safely, on August 20th, 1561, to the harbour of Leith and her native land.   She was not yet nineteen years old.

The state to which the Catholic Church in Scotland had been reduced a year later is vividly given by Nicholas Goudanus, a Dutch Jesuit, who was sent to Mary as a nuncio of Pope Pius IV, in a letter to the General of the Society.

"The aspect of things," he writes,[1] "is miserable

[1] From a translation by Father Forbes-Leith in *Narratives of Scottish Catholics.*

74

enough. The monasteries are nearly all in ruins, some completely destroyed; churches, altars, sanctuaries, are overthrown and profaned. The images of Christ and of the saints are broken and lying in the dust. No religious rite is celebrated in any part of the kingdom, no Mass ever said in public except in the Queen's chapel, and none of the sacraments are publicly administered with Catholic ceremonial. Children can be baptized only after the heretical form, and that on Sundays only, so that many infants die unbaptized. The ministers, as they call them, are either apostate monks or laymen of low rank, and are quite unlearned, being cobblers, shoemakers, tanners, or the like, while their ministrations consist merely of declamation against the Supreme Pontiff, and the holy sacrifice of the altar, the idolatry of the Mass, worship of images, and invocation of saints. These, and other impieties, they are continually shouting into the ears of the credulous multitude, who know no better. They are so insane as not only to have destroyed the images of the saints, but also burnt the writings of the holy fathers of the Church, thus repudiating the authority of general councils and apostolic tradition. They reverence nothing but Holy Scripture, and this they interpret in a sense as opposite as possible to the doctrines of the Church. They have superintendents, who diligently visit the churches, drive out by force the legitimate pastors wherever they find any, and not only confirm the wretched people in their errors, but draw away Catholics, and sometimes even priests, from the true religion. One day, close to the place where I lodged, three priests publicly abjured the Catholic faith; and another time, while I was there, one of the principal superintendents, a doctor of theology and a monk, then about seventy years of age, was openly married. This was done to enforce practically, as he had often done verbally, their doctrine of the unlawfulness of the vow of chastity, which they are perpetually proclaiming from the pulpit. They use every possible device to lead the wretched people astray. Whenever any one comes into a court of law, the magistrates always inquire first if they are ' Papists,' or belong to their congregation. Should they be Papists, they can get very little, if any, attention paid to their cause. The men in power acknowledge the queen's title, but prevent her exercising any of the rights of sovereignty : whenever her opinion does not agree with theirs, they oppose her at once. Not only so, but they deceive her as well, and frighten her with threats of an English invasion, especially when she is meditating any steps in support of her faith, reminding her that the English did really invade Scotland three years ago, at the time when her mother, of pious memory, endeavoured to shake off her heretical tyrants with the aid of the French. What can this good young princess effect, brought up amid the splendour and luxury of the French Court, scarcely twenty years old, and destitute of all human support and counsel? Her very confessor abandoned her just before I came away, and returned to France with some of her Catholic attendants, leaving her alone among heretics, whom, notwithstanding, she continues to resist and counteract to the best of her power."

This gloomy picture enhances respect for the courage and sincerity of a priest like Ninian Winzet who at such a time dared to dispute openly with the preachers. Winzet had been master of the grammar-school in Linlithgow and provost of the Collegiate Church of St Michael, but when called upon to sign the Protestant Confession he refused, was deprived of his office, and forced to leave the "kindly toun" of Linlithgow. He went to live in Edinburgh and in February 1562, addressed "four scoir thre questions" to Knox, challenging him to reply in writing. A summary [1] is worth reprinting.

The Protestants are asked, among other questions: Whether they believe the judgment of the Holy Church to be set forth most truly by the primitive doctors and general councils, or by John Calvin and

[1] Grub: *Ecclesiastical History*, Vol. II, pp. 117–19.

his associates? Why they have taken away the true meaning of the article of the Creed, that Christ descended into hell, substituting for it Calvin's private opinion that the words signify only the anguish which Christ suffered? Why they make their two sacraments signs only of salvation whereby men are assured of God's grace, and not rather efficacious means whereby God works His grace in them? Why, since they admit of no ceremonies except such as are expressly commanded in Scripture, they notwithstanding refuse to baptize children unless their father holds them up before the pulpit? Why they baptize in the church only, and not in the field, or by the river-side, like St John Baptist and St Philip? Why they baptize not unless the child then receive a name? Why their table is covered with a white cloth at the Communion? Why they cause others than the minister to distribute the bread and the wine, when our Saviour alone did so to the apostles, commanding them as His ministers to do the same? Why they make their Communion before dinner, when the sacrament was instituted after supper? Why they refuse to solemnize matrimony unless the banns are first proclaimed? Why they cause persons about to be married to take each other by the hand, and sometimes a ring to be given? Why they say that in the Communion nothing is present except bread and wine, when our Saviour

says expressly, " This is my body ; this is my blood " ?
Why they do not minister the Communion to the
sick before they depart out of this life ?   Why, when
their sovereign Lady Mary has shown such humility,
gentleness, and wisdom, as should soften the heart
of every true Scot, they exhort her subjects so fervently
to rebellion unless she accept the opinions of Calvin ?
Since by elders in the New Testament are meant
bishops and priests, whose office it is to preach and
minister the sacraments, why they have invented a
new order of elders, who are forbidden to discharge
these offices ?   Since the sacrament of confirmation
was used by the apostles, why do they esteem it a
thing of no importance, and but papistical superstition ?   Since the priests of the Church should come
to the sick and anoint them with oil, and pray for
them, as our Saviour teaches by the mouth of St
James, why have they abolished extreme unction, and
deprived it of the name of a sacrament ?   Although it
is well known that in the primitive Church married
persons were often promoted to be bishops, priests,
and deacons, where was it ever heard in that Church
that men, unmarried at the time of their ordination,
were allowed to marry afterwards without reproof
and punishment ?   Since in the Scriptures we read
of care bestowed on the funerals of the patriarchs, of
our Lord, of St John the Baptist, and of St Stephen,

why have they dishonoured the bodies and sepulchres of the princes and nobles of Scotland? Since they admit no unwritten tradition, why do they celebrate their Sabbath-day with the Catholics on Sunday, and not with the Jews on Saturday? Why do they use, as Catholics do, to sing Glory to the Father, and to the Son, and to the Holy Ghost, at the end of every psalm, when that godly form was commanded by Pope Damasus to be sung for the rebuke of heretics? What can they show expressly written to confute the Anabaptists of error, who deny that children should be baptized in infancy? What Scripture have they for receiving so many gospels and epistles in the New Testament, and no more? If the Church be invisible, how can men show their complaints to the Church, according to our Saviour's command, and how in that case, can the Church be the pillar and ground of the truth? Since fasting was practised by Moses, Elias, and the Ninevites, by St John the Baptist, and by our Saviour, who also foretold that His disciples should fast when the Bridegroom was removed, how is the Church guilty of idolatry in observing the yearly fast of Lent, and the weekly fasts of Friday, and Wednesday or Saturday? Why have they rejected the monastic life, which was held in such estimation by the primitive Church? Why have they thrown down the monasteries, which by a godly reformation

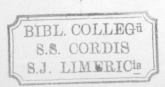

might have nourished men given to prayer, and been colleges of learning for the support of poor students? or, if the monasteries were polluted with idolatry, why have they not destroyed wholly, as they have done in part, the parish churches and cathedrals, in which the same idolatry (so-called) was practised? Since the Scriptures mention the frequent prayers of our Lord and His apostles, of David, and of Daniel, was it not a goodly rule of the Church that prayers should be sung or read seven times daily by able ministers chosen thereto; and why do they in their Reformed order pray only by one minister, once only every other day in the best churches, in many places thrice a-week, and in far more not once a-month?

Knox replied with a sermon. Winzet demanded an answer in writing. Knox replied with another sermon, in which he compared himself to the prophet Amos. Winzet argued against the validity of the comparison, with some damaging illustrations from both Testaments. Knox would not or could not reply. At Easter there were riots in Edinburgh when the magistrates tried to stop any observance of the festival. In May Winzet published *Certane Tractatis for Reformatioun of Doctryne and Maneris set forth at the desyre and in the name of the afflictit Catholikis of inferiour ordour of Clergie and layit men in Scotland.*

The first tract denounces the moral laxity of the

higher clergy and calls upon them to rise from their
ignoble sleep :

" O merciful God, what deadly sleep is this that
has oppressed you, that in so great uproar, tumult,
and terrible clamour, ye waken not forth of your
dream ? And in so great danger of death, ye have
no regard of your own lives nor others ? Awake,
awake, we say, and put to your hands stoutly to save
Peter's ship ; for he neither sleeps nor slumbers who
beholds all your doings, and sees your thoughts, but
shall require the blood out of your hands of the
smallest one that shall perish through your negligence."

He then turns upon the nobles, " who, lifted up in
high curiosity of questions, and (as appears to us) in
manifest errors and presumption, make of the Gospel
a taking craft, without further practice of God's law
in deed ; who, although they cry out fast upon
idolatry, yet they are, no less than the other degenerate
ignorants above specified, as wicked Ethnicks and
bound subjects to the monstrous idolatry of avarice,
never intending to cleanse their hands of the kirk
rents, nor of the blood and sweat of the poor ; spurring
others to reformation, but indeed never reforming
themselves from the idolatry of avarice."

He impressively concludes in words addressed to
the Queen, " we intending to be faithful Christians,
and ready to suffer they Grace's laws for any crime

committed by us, are compelled either to affirm in religion before man contrary to our conscience, or to be incarcerated or exiled, and holden by the world as infidels, heretics, apostates, or wicked persons, unworthy the company of Christians; and in the meantime, at such extreme poverty are all we of the clergy, that we are almost lost without any mercy of man. The other cause is that we being of small learning, and so loath to be hypocrites to our condemnation, have long abided for reasoning of the bishops, theologians, and others well learned, to a godly reformation right necessary. Which thing not coming to pass, but more had of the kitchen than of the choir, we may no longer contain us, but express on all sides as we think, referring our judgment to the holy Catholic Kirk."

The second tract challenges the " lauchfull Vocatioun of Johne Knox, and his Brether Precheouris," and the final tract impeaches the " Provost, Baillies, and Counsell of Edinburgh " for their treatment of Easter and other holy feasts.

Knox continued to shirk answering Winzet, who in July published *The Last Blast of the Trumpet of Godis Worde aganis the usurpit auctorite of Johne Knox and his Calvinian brethren*. Knox, unable to answer this champion effectively, invoked the aid of the magistrates. The printing press was seized, the printer imprisoned, and all the copies of the pamphlet destroyed. It was intended to arrest the audacious author himself, but he escaped from the country to live out the rest of his life in exile. In 1577 he became abbot of the Benedictine monastery of St James at Ratisbon. Here says the *Dictionary of National Biography*, " he revived this ancient decayed seminary of learning, and by introducing the old Scots method of instruction soon restored its celebrity." So it would seem that Scots education does not date from John Knox. In 1592 Ninian Winzet died at the age of seventy-four, renowned for the virtue of his life, the profundity of his learning, and the shrewdness of his polemical method.

Knox's reputation as a " Calvinian " champion may have suffered a set-back by his clear defeat at the hands of Winzet, for in the autumn of 1562 he tackled the aged Abbot Quintin Kennedy of Crossraguel in the last public disputation of this nature recorded, the subject being the sacrifice of the Mass. Knox claimed the victory, crowing out his usual indecent exultation over his opponents in a prologue to a printed version of the argument; but it is noteworthy that no more public disputations were held, and we have direct testimony that he cut a very poor figure beside the worthy old abbot.

It is beyond the scope of these pages to attempt

even an outline of the treacheries and bloody deeds by which a collection of the blackest villains that ever defiled the pages of history drove the Queen of Scots from her throne to find captivity and death at the hands of a queen who lacked at once the essential bodily and mental characteristics of womanhood.

Equally beyond the scope of these pages is any attempt to trace in detail the process by which that same collection of traitors and murderers consolidated the work of the Reformation in Scotland.

Yet the Faith endured. In May 1569 four priests of Dunblane were seized for the crime of saying Mass and sentenced to be hanged at Stirling. The Regent Moray, who had just been burning witches in Dundee and St Andrews, commuted the death-penalty, but ordered the condemned priests to be chained to the market-cross in their vestments with chalice and missal in their hands. Here for an hour they were pelted by the mob with rotten eggs and " uther villany " after which their vestments and missals were burnt by the hangman and they themselves were banished. This kind of scene was frequently repeated elsewhere in the country.

Moray and Knox would appear to have drawn close together at this time, and it looks as if they were plotting to gain the crown for Moray. The Bastard approached Elizabeth with the suggestion that his sister should be handed over to him, adding a sinister promise that her life should not be shortened by any undue means. He was so eager for his sister's body that on January 2nd, 1570, he sent a secret agent to offer to surrender to Elizabeth the Earl of Northumberland, who had fled to Scotland after the luckless northern rising, in exchange for Mary. On the very same day Knox wrote to Cecil:

" Benefits of God's hands received, crave that men be thankful; and danger known would be avoided. *If ye strike not at the root, the branches that appear to be broken will bud again,* and that more quickly than men can believe, with greater force than we could wish. Turn your een unto your God; forget yourself and yours, when consultation is to be had in matters of such weight as presently ly upon you. Albeit I have been fremedly handled, yet was I never enemy to the quietness of England. God grant you wisdom. In haste, of Edinburgh, the second of Janur. Yours to command in God, John Knox, with his one foot in the grave."

After that direct incitement to murder the unhappy Queen he had so long hated and tortured, one could fancy, without too culpable a prejudice, that the other foot of John Knox was in Hell.

Three weeks later, in the middle of his last dark intrigue, the Bastard was shot in Linlithgow by

Hamilton of Bothwellhaugh. He was cold and supple as a snake, stealthy and silent as a snake, merciless as a snake, and like a snake he bit with poisoned fangs the sister who had warmed him against her heart. Moray was succeeded by a lesser villain, Lennox, the father of Darnley, who made haste to hang his chief opponent the Archbishop of St Andrews. The tolerance of John Hamilton was too often weakness. He had an amiable character, but the times were too violent for him, and the Hamiltons were always a weak ambiguous race. Lennox was killed a few months later in an engagement between his troops and some of the Queen's supporters under Huntly. He was succeeded by the Earl of Mar, who continued the intrigue with Elizabeth which Moray had started. Elizabeth promised to surrender her captive to the new Regent on condition that she was to be put to death immediately. Killigrew, the envoy she despatched to arrange matters, had an interview with Knox, and to judge by the letter he wrote to Burghley he had obtained Knox's approval of the intended crime. However, as if the patience of Almighty God could no longer brook these instruments He had chosen to chastise His degenerate Church, Mar died as suddenly as his two predecessors, in October 1572. He was a most distinguished traitor. His Queen had given him rank and honour, and made him guardian of the infant

Prince James. He rewarded her by bearing that infant Prince to the field of battle as an encouragement to the rebels. He had even tried in the vilest way to turn that child's love to hate by allowing his mother to be vilely slandered in his presence. He was of course a bulwark of the Reformation and a pensioner of England. The Earl of Mar was succeeded as Regent by the Earl of Morton, who was elected on the day of John Knox's death.

Of late years the character of the father of the Scottish Reformation has come to seem less admirable, and there has been an inclination to regard him as a somewhat embarrassing patriarch of the Established Kirk. Yet if we consider the attributes of Presbyterianism from its origin until the present day it will be difficult to deprive John Knox of the fame he deserves as its true begetter, and of the honour of being one of its most thoroughly typical exponents. It was he who carried the theory of the Elect to its logical conclusion by ascribing to the Elect those privileges in the matter of Divine favouritism which had once belonged to the Jews. It was he who first implanted in the Scottish mind the belief that worldly success and material prosperity were the visible tokens of God's pleasure in His Elect. Indeed, it would hardly be too much to suggest that it was he who first presented England to the Scotsman as the promised land of Canaan, flowing with milk and honey. There is no doubt that if he could have had his way with the Established Church over the border he would have been content to achieve the Reformation in Scotland by the absorption of his country into England. He was always an Anglicizing influence, and one of Ninian Winzet's objections to him was his inability to write in good Scots.

" Gif ze throw curiositie of nouationis hes forzet our auld plane Scottis quwhilk zour mother lerit zou, in tymes cuming I sall wryte zou my mynd in Latin, for I am nocht acquyntit with zour Southeroun," he jeered at the Protestant champion.

Knox's first wife was an Englishwoman. His brother was a trader in England, settled in Preston. His sons were sent to Cambridge, and one of them became Vicar of Clacton in Essex. It is true that Knox refused an English bishopric ; but when he was taunted with being offended at not being offered one of the proposed Scots bishoprics he boasted that he had refused a much more important episcopal dignity in England.

We are unfortunate in knowing so little of Knox's early years. In them would probably be found the key to the character we meet already fixed at forty years of age. It would be easier to account for the extravagance of his denunciation if he actually ever had been ordained to the priesthood, for in that case the consciousness of the need to justify his apostasy would always have been urgent. That he was in minor orders is all we can know for sure. He was a man of abounding self-conceit. When in the year before his death he assisted at a play in St Andrews which represented the capture of the castle according to "Mr Knox's doctrine," it must have been his vanity that overcame his disapproval of mummery. His hatred of Mary of Guise, of Mary Stuart, indeed of almost every human creature he particularly hated, is usually to be traced to the preacher's offended vanity. His vitality was prodigious. That at the age of sixty he could take as a second wife a girl of sixteen and beget upon her three daughters, however repugnant it may be to a sense of decency, is certainly a tribute to such vitality. It is the combination of vanity with vitality which so often induces in the natural coward the self-assertiveness that strives to mask the cowardice. In Knox's case cowardice is so obvious that we may suspect Morton of a sardonic jest quite in keeping with his character when at Knox's funeral he spoke this epitaph, "Here lieth one who in his life never feared the face of man." Several instances have been given already of the Reformer's cowardice, and the weakness was constant with him to the end. After the murder of Rizzio cowardice played on the guilty conscience of an accomplice to make him run from Edinburgh at the news that the Queen was advancing on the city with 8000 troops. After making himself scarce in the west, he obtained leave from the Assembly to pay a judicious visit to England whence he returned to preach boldly in favour of an English alliance only after the Queen was incarcerated in Loch Leven. In 1571 he fell out with his old confederate, Kirkcaldy of Grange, who as Governor of Edinburgh Castle, was threatening Knox with bodily violence. Safe in St Andrews, the champion of Presbyterianism against the modified Episcopacy which it was proposed to introduce, wrote to the brethren in Edinburgh, exhorting them to " watch for the preservation of another without grudging or murmuring. From the pulpit he threatened Kirkcaldy mightily in " that Babylon the Castle of Edinburgh." Knox's ranting eloquence was received with such lack of appreciation in St Andrews, that it may account for the tone of that letter to the General Assembly in Perth in which he urges them " above all things to preserve the kirk from the bondage of the universities." Thus the vanity persists to the end; and it was strong enough to overcome his fear of Kirkcaldy's sword when he was invited to return to St Giles's as minister with assurances that he would be allowed to attack from the pulpit his enemies in the Castle. But he was not to live much longer, and he spent his last days in the November of 1572, alternating between expressions of devotion to God and savage denunciation of his enemies. To Kirkcaldy he sent word that he should be " disgracefully dragged from his nest to punishment and hung on a gallows in the face of the sun." Then, calling upon his Saviour to receive his spirit, John Knox died.

Fifteen weary years later the royal victim of his insane and murderous hate, no further to be touched by treason, steel or poison, by malice domestic or foreign levy, yet denied even upon the fearful edge of eternity the outward consolations of her faith, appealed to that Saviour:

> O Domine Deus, speravi in Te,
> O care mi Jesu, nunc libera me.
> In dura catena, in misera poena, desidero Te.
> Languendo, dolendo, et genuflectendo
> Adoro, imploro, ut liberes me.

Well might the Archbishop of Bourges, preaching in the Cathedral of Notre Dame the funeral oration of the martyred Queen of Scots, exclaim : [1]

" Marie accusée, accusée de quel crime ! accusée d'estre Catholique ! Heureux crime ! desirable accusation ! "

---

[1] *Oraison funèbre de Marie, royne d'Escosse.* Paris, 1588.

CHAPTER V

THE Earl of Morton's ecclesiastical policy as Regent was to bring the Established Scottish Church as nearly as possible into line with the Established English Church in accordance with his profound admiration for Elizabeth. The head of the Presbyterian opposition to even the kind of modified episcopacy Morton advocated was Andrew Melville, whose impetuous leadership but logical readiness to face the influence of his ecclesiastical theories upon the general conduct of the State and people may be considered primarily responsible for the characteristically Scottish form of Calvinism, so pathetic in its revelation of individual frailty, so tragic in its effect upon the general frailty of human nature. At the same time, Melville was an ardent Anglicizer and worked strenuously to obtain a legislative union between the two countries. He had the self-importance of the little man ; but he seems to have been devoid of personal ambition, which distinguishes him from almost every one of the early Reformers. He was elected Moderator at the General Assembly of 1578. The modified bishops were soon put in their place, and after a series of derogatory enactments the whole episcopalian system was abolished in 1580.

During the Moderatorship of Melville the *Second Book of Discipline* was published, but it was not sanctioned by Parliament. In this exalted claims were made for the Presbyterian Kirk at the expense of the civil powers whose authority had been recognized by the *First Book of Discipline*. These exalted claims were to lead to the fierce and bloody struggles for supremacy during the seventeenth century between state-aided episcopacy preaching the Divine right of Kings and a combination of democratic and theocratic authority which went even beyond the most arrogant Papal claims in the Middle Ages.

The enmity of the Kirk contributed to the fall of Morton who was beheaded in 1581 by the Halifax Maiden he had introduced. The leaders of the Reformation were dying off fast. George Buchanan went in 1582. The only good thing about him was his Latin. Next year Sir James Balfour, one of the conspirators against Beaton, whom contemporary opinion regarded as the most unscrupulous knave of them all, followed Buchanan to the grave.

It is impossible to attempt any estimate of the numerical strength of Catholics twenty-five years after the Reformation had been imposed; but the continuous state of panic in which the Protestants lived suggests that the possibility of a Catholic reaction was still a real menace. Dauntless Jesuit missionaries, avid for martyrdom, were reaching Scotland from time to time and administering the Sacraments to the faithful denied their own priests by the rigorous persecution. Many distinguished Scotsmen were being reconciled to the Church. The murder of the Queen of Scots at Fotheringay roused for a while the old hatred of England, and King James was sufficiently shaken by the evidence of popular disapproval to appoint the exiled Archbishop Beaton of Glasgow to be his ambassador in France. The Catholic lords in the North were in communication with various continental powers, and if the traditional dependence on France had been boldly sacrificed to a closer co-operation with Spain, the Armada might have sailed to the advantage of Scotland. As it was, Huntly nearly persuaded James to throw open the Scottish ports to Philip's fleet. However, Melville concentrated the Presbyterian opposition to assist England, and the chance to avenge the Queen of Scots and fling Elizabeth from her throne upon the dustheap of history was lost.

In any case, perhaps James was too anxious to succeed to the English throne to run any risks, for he allowed Elizabeth to buy him off with a pension of five thousand pounds a year from any attempt to avenge his mother. Still, it was a critical moment for Protestantism. The ministers were crying out for steps to be taken to stop " the defection of the multitude from the truth " and the " erection of the idolatrie of the Masse in diverse quarters of the land." In Stirling itself we hear of " superstitious ceremonies, pilgrimages, and Christ's wells, fasting, bainfyres (bonfires on feasts), girdls (blest scapulars), carrels, and such lyke." [1]

In 1593 all Jesuits, seminary priests, and excommunicated persons [2] were ordered by royal proclamation to leave Edinburgh within three hours, on pain of death. This step was provoked by the capture of George Kerr, who under torture, had revealed the negotiations between the Catholic lords and Spain. The Earl of Angus and Lord Fintry were implicated, and Fintry was put to death because he would not buy his pardon with his apostasy. " He answered very resolutely that it would be a bad bargain for him if he were to prefer earth to Heaven." [3]

A month or two later the Assembly petitioned the King to take various severe measures against priests, and demanded that all persons found by the Kirk to be Papists should be debarred from office, from

---

[1] *Booke of the Universall Kirke.*

[2] Mostly persons who had outwardly conformed to the Kirk, but kept up when possible their Catholic duties.

[3] Barberini MSS.

access to the King, and from the protection of the laws of the realm. In 1594 James despatched an expedition under the Earl of Argyll to ravage the Gordon country with fire and sword. The Earls of Huntly and Errol with an inferior force defeated Argyll at Glenlivet; but the King with Andrew Melville and a crowd of ministers led an army up to Aberdeen, and the Catholic rally was dispersed. Huntly and Errol skulked in the Highlands for a while, but at last resolved to leave the country. Father Gordon, the uncle of Huntly, said Mass for the last time in the Cathedral of Elgin, calling upon the faint hearts to remain and venture everything for their faith. Yet in March 1595 they quitted Scotland.

Two years later they returned with the Earl of Angus, and in order to save their estates from confiscation subscribed to the Confession of Faith and recanted their errors. Their apostasy was a great shock to their fellow-Catholics, temporary though it turned out to be.

Perhaps it was the conversion to Catholicism of the Queen, Anne of Denmark, which led to such high hopes of James's own conversion; but it is difficult to suppose that there was ever any likelihood of it. Nevertheless, he was suspected of Catholic leanings, and the Gunpowder Plot was a wonderfully well-engineered piece of propaganda to put a Catholic reaction in England outside any possible attainment. To this day it is difficult to convince people that the Gunpowder conspirators fell into the trap of a cunning statesman.

However, during the decade before James obtained his heart's desire by ascending the English throne after Elizabeth's horror-haunted death, the King of Scotland had made up his mind that Presbyterianism was a threat to monarchy, and the strife between that system of church government and episcopalianism occupies the arena.

As early as 1584, the King had forced through Parliament various statutes which told heavily against Andrew Melville and his Presbyterian following. " The royal authority over all estates, spiritual as well as temporal, was confirmed ; to decline the jurisdiction of the King and Council was declared to be treason ; all conventions, whether civil or ecclesiastical, held without the sovereign's licence, were forbidden ; and power was given to the Archbishop of St Andrews, the bishops, and other commissioners, to take order in matters ecclesiastical within their dioceses, to visit the churches and ministers of the same, to reform the colleges, and to give collation of benefices." [1]

James was trying to bring his realm of Scotland into accord with that realm of England, to the peaceful possession of which he was looking forward as eagerly as a poor relation to a rich legacy.

[1] Grub : *Ecclesiastical History*, Vol. III, p. 255.

The struggle was protracted. In 1592 the Presbyterians regained some of their privileges, but James feared their seditious influence and would not give them an inch more than he could help. In 1596, a minister called Black preached a violent sermon, denouncing Elizabeth as an atheist and the religion of England as an empty show. He proclaimed that Satan ruled both Court and Council, that all kings were devil's bairns, that the Lords of Session were miscreants, the nobles cormorants, and Elizabeth herself a woman from whom it was vain to hope for any good thing. Black was supported by the Edinburgh preachers when he refused to appear before the Council, and an attempt was made to persuade Lord Hamilton to rebel and claim the throne.

In March 1600 James secured from the General Assembly meeting at Montrose an acknowledgement of his right to nominate bishops from lists of names submitted by the Kirk; but, three or four months later, the Gowrie plot, which was certainly abetted by the ministers, did not make him feel more tolerant of Presbyterianism. In his treatise on Government, *Basilikon Doron*, addressed to his son, the King let fly. "Take heed to such Puritans," he wrote, "very pests in the Church and Commonweal, whom no deserts can oblige, neither oaths nor promises bind, aspiring without measure, railing without reason. I protest before the great God, that ye shall never find with any Highland or Border thieves greater ingratitude, and more lies and vile perjuries than with these fanatic spirits." [1]

What had these fanatical spirits, sometimes in alliance with hungry nobles and insensate mobs, sometimes with the help of Parliament, King, and Council, achieved for Scotland during the forty years which had elapsed since the Reformation?

They had driven out the priests, and starved the faithful of the Sacraments save when they could be administered by devoted missionaries under peril of death. They had destroyed the great sanctuaries, and turned the smaller sanctuaries to purposes for which their builders had never intended them. They had enjoyed the prestige of material success. They had had many years in which to bring up the younger generation according to their own religious notions that they might show an example to the rest of Christendom of the benefits of evangelical simplicity. There should have been fair fruits by now from the snowy blossoms of the Reformed doctrines and the Reformed worship. What were those fruits? We must avoid the faintest shadow of prejudice by convicting the Reformed Church out of the mouths of its own ministers.

Here is what the General Assembly of 1596 has to

1 Βασιλικὸν Δῶρον. p. 89.

observe about the state of Scotland thirty-six years after the Reformation :

" An universal coldness, want of zeal, ignorance, contempt of the Word ; prayer, singing of psalms, and the Word of God profaned and abused ; superstition and idolatry entertained ; blaspheming of God's name ; swearing, banning, and cursing ; profanation of the Sabbath by working, journeying, trysting, gaming, dancing, drinking, fishing, killing, and milling ; inferiors not doing duty to superiors ; children having pleas of law against their parents, and marrying without their consent ; breaches of duty betwixt married persons ; great bloodshed ; deadly feuds, and assisting bloodshedders to elude the laws ; fornications, adulteries, incests, unlawful marriages, and divorcements ; excessive drinking and gluttony ; filthy and impure speeches and songs ; sacrilege in all estates growing daily, to the utter undoing of the Kirk ; cruel oppression of the poor ; thraldom in service ; oppression by usury ; lying ; universal neglect of justice ; judges ignorant and profane. Through the abusing, delaying, perverting, neglecting of justice, murder, oppression, adultery, incest, and all horrible crimes abound. Besides the kirks in Argyll and the Isles, there are four hundred kirks wanting ministers, whereby the people perish in ignorance, atheism, and profanity."

The fruits of the Reformation seem to have rotted with exceeding swiftness.

It might have been supposed that the strife between Episcopalians and Presbyterians would have relaxed the rigour of the persecution of Catholics; but on the contrary this was intensified after James united the Crowns. No doubt the eagerness of the Presbyterians to accuse the Episcopalians of encouraging Popery by their nearness to purge Scotland of Calvinism excited the Episcopalians to demonstrate their own evangelical fervour by the harshness of their attitude toward Catholics. The martyrdom of the Jesuit Father John Ogilvie was an instance of this anti-Papal zeal.

John Ogilvie had been working less than a year on the Scottish mission when in October 1614 he was denounced in Glasgow for saying Mass, and arrested. Some letters presumed to incriminate him politically were discovered, and he was severely interrogated at first in Glasgow and again in Edinburgh where he was tortured by denial of sleep until " his braines became lightsome " and he was said to have revealed the names of some of his accomplices. The King commissioned Archbishop Spottiswood and others to examine Ogilvie upon his beliefs about the royal prerogative, but whether he was actually tortured at this examination is not clear. We have Spottiswood's own testimony that he suggested torture, but that the King " would not have these forms used with men of his profession." If Ogilvie were merely found to be a Jesuit he was to be banished, but if he was inculpated in stirring up rebellion ordinary justice was to take its course. The trial was held in Glasgow, and in the indictment Ogilvie was told that he was being tried for denying the King's authority, not for saying Mass. The Presbyterian historian Calderwood significantly thought that such an indictment " seemed rather a hindrance to the execution of justice upon the persons presently guiltie then to mean in earnest the repressing of Papists." Calderwood need not have worried himself. The steadfast priest never showed the slightest inclination to escape the penalty by taking advantage of the King's desire to concentrate upon the political aspect of his case. He was asked by Spottis-wood if he would make any attempt to return to Scotland should he be banished instead of being sentenced to death. " If I should be exiled for any evil deed committed," Ogilvie answered, " I should certainly take care not to come back ; but if I were exiled for this cause which I sustain, I should not fail to retrace my steps to the country. And would that every hair of my head might convert a thousand to the orthodox faith, and you, archbishop, in the first place."

Pressed upon his attitude toward the Royal prerogative, Ogilvie defiantly replied : " If the King will be to me as his predecessors were to mine, I will obey . . . but, if he do otherwise, and play the runagate from God, as he and you all do, I will not acknowledge him more than this old hat."

The Jesuit was found guilty, and three hours later he was led out to the scaffold to be hanged.

Archbishop Spottiswood, who was translated from the see of Glasgow to St Andrews a month or two after the death of Ogilvie, may be considered a typical example of the Erastian churchmen who stood at the backs of James VI and Charles I. Convinced of the evils of what he called " parity " in the Kirk, Spottiswood's ecclesiastical career was devoted to securing the recognition of the Royal prerogative, the destruction of the claims of the ministers to dictate to the nation in civil affairs and the gradual introduction of a more formal style of public worship. He perceived the threat to true Scottish independence in the attempted assimilation of the Established Kirk to the Established Church of England; but his Erastian principles did not allow him to offer any effective resistance to the policy of his royal masters. Although he foresaw the popular fury that the attempt in 1637 to impose the Book of Common Prayer was to rouse, he did not shirk what he believed to be his duty. After the revival of the National Covenant in 1638 Spottiswood's life was in danger, and on his retiring across the Border to Newcastle he was deposed by the Assembly on the charge of "profaning the Sabbath, carding and diceing, riding through the country the whole day, tippling and drinking in taverns till midnight, falsifying the acts of the Aberdeen Assembly, lying and slandering the old Assembly and Covenant in his wicked book (*A History of the Church and State of Scotland*), of adultery, incest, sacrilege, and frequent simony."

These charges appear for the most part to be nothing more than the frothy ravings of religious phrenzy; but they are melancholy evidence of the mental condition of the Covenanters. A year later Spottiswood died, and was buried with much ceremony in Westminster Abbey.

If it was possible for the General Assembly of the Kirk to spatter with such rabid foam an Established Archbishop, the foulness of the controversial methods employed against Catholics may easily be imagined; and when we contemplate that immense midden of lies added to year by year over more than three centuries we cannot feel, unhappily, the least astonishment that in the year 1935 the guttersnipes of Protestantism are still nosing in that midden for the vilest offensive missiles.

CHAPTER VI

IN 1598 the secular priests of the Scottish mission were placed under the jurisdiction of George Blackwell, the archpriest at the head of the English mission, and to the discontent thus caused may partially be attributed the formation of the Scots College in Rome by Pope Clement VIII in 1600. The Scots College in Paris went back to the times of Bruce, and in 1576 Dr Cheyne, formerly parish priest of Aboyne, had founded a small Scots seminary at Tournai. From Tournai this seminary was moved to Lorraine, and administered by Scottish members of the Society of Jesus. The next move was to Douai in 1593 whence three years later it moved to Louvain, from there in 1609 to Antwerp, returning finally to Douai in 1612. Besides the priests trained at these seminaries, missionaries came from the Scottish Benedictine monasteries of Wärzburg and Ratisbon, the only two of the numerous Scottish monasteries in Germany during the Middle Ages which still had Scottish monks.

The administration of the English archpriests was succeeded in 1623 of a vicar-apostolic for England and

Scotland who was appointed Bishop of Chalcedon *in partibus*. The Scottish Catholics, whatever the wretchedness of their condition, could not stand the notion of being under the jurisdiction of an English bishop, and petitioned Pope Clement VIII to be withdrawn from it. This memorial insisted upon the old enmity between Scotland and England and the old struggle to keep the hands of the Archbishop of York off the Scottish sees. No doubt the fact that the English vicar-apostolic had no desire for authority over the Scottish priests helped. At any rate, they were withdrawn from his jurisdiction and put back under that of their own missionary prefects. During most of the seventeenth century the priests serving the Scottish mission, regular or secular, were few enough, and the Catholic who knows the warmth of gratitude with which thousands of the sacrament-starved faithful in the Highlands and Islands responded to any effort that was made to reach them cannot but feel some bitterness in the thought of what might have been done if only the Scottish mission had been well organized and financed by the Congregation of Propaganda, and left less dependent on the irregular enterprise of devoted individuals.

The furious struggle between the Episcopalians and Presbyterians which devastated Scotland as much materially as spiritually left a desert of opportunities for the replanting of which it is difficult to believe that the Catholic missionaries took the fullest advantage. Yet from the comparative security of the present it is all too easy to criticize, and when we consider the hell of hate in which seventeenth-century Scotland existed we cannot blame the Roman authorities if they did seem to give way to the languor of despair. When one reads of the scene in St Giles's provoked by the harridan Jenny Geddes one seems to be reading about a nation of lunatics. The Catholics were involved in the popular hostility to the Episcopalians. Popery and Prelacy became synonymous. Yet Charles I, like his father before him, had tried to demonstrate the undefiled Protestantism of his Episcopalian ambitions by an added severity against Catholics. One of the cruellest measures of the persecution was the taking away of their children from prominent Catholics in order to have them compulsorily educated as Protestants. In 1631, for instance, the Earl of Nithsdale was ordered by the council to hand over his young son Lord Maxwell " for his breeding and education in the true religion." The harrying of the Catholics became so merciless that in 1633 Pope Urban VIII wrote to Queen Henrietta Maria, exhorting her intervention. The King seems to have made several feeble attempts to obtain leniency in the case of individuals, but the ferocious activity of the Presbyterian ministers was too much for him. Examples are all too unhappily numerous, but the case of Robert Rigg of Dumfries will serve as typical. In 1634 he was charged by the Presbytery with getting himself married "by a Popish priest, on a Sunday, at night with candle-light, above the Bridge of Cluden in the fields, in presence of four witnesses, to Elspeth Maxwell, an excommunicate Papist." The minister of Dumfries, one Thomas Ramsay, appeared in person before the Council to press the charge. Rigg was sentenced to be imprisoned indefinitely in the Edinburgh Tolbooth, and his wife was shut up in the gaol with fourteen other women, wives of tradesmen, accused of hearing Mass during the past year.

Nor were people the only objects of the Kirk's fervid Christianity. In 1640 the General Assembly dealt with the offence of some monuments of ancient piety left in Aberdeen. "They ordained our blessed Lord Jesus Christ his arms to be cut out of the forefront of the pulpit thereof. . . . And besides, where there was any crucifixes set in glass windows, those he (the Master of Forbes) caused pull out. . . . He caused a mason strike out Christ's arms in hewn rock, on each end of Bishop Gavin Dunbar's tomb, and siklike chisel out the name of Jesus, drawn cipher-ways, out of the timber wall on the foreside of Machar's aisle. . . .

The crucifix on the Old Town Cross was thrown down; the crucifix on the New Toun Cross closed up, being loth to break the stone; the crucifix on the west end of St Nicholas' Church in New Aberdeen thrown down, whilk was never touched before." [1]

A few months later some Covenanters smashed up the painted wooden screen in the Cathedral of Elgin.

" On the west side," says the writer already quoted, " was painted in excellent colours, illuminate with stars of bright gold, the crucifixion of our Lord and Saviour Jesus Christ; and this piece was so excellently done, that the colours and stars never faded nor vanished, but kept hale and sound as they were at the beginning. . . . On the other side of the wall, towards the east, was drawn the Day of Judgment. . . . It was said this minister caused bring home to his house the timber thereof, and burn the same for kitchen and other uses."

In that same year the Jesuit Father James Mambrecht was writing on December 17th:

" Within the last ten days, orders have been published throughout Scotland not to sell anything to Catholics, or buy anything of them. Many are already deprived of their rents and income. Several Catholics have offered three-fourths of their property, provided they may keep the remaining fourth for the

---

[1] Spalding : *History of the Troubles in Scotland*, 1624–1645.

maintenance of themselves and their families, and even this is refused. Nay, our adversaries impiously swear that not a single Catholic shall live or remain in Scotland by the end of the year. . . . A noble baron, seventy years old and more, was seized in England, and brought to Edinburgh, whose family they ruined, whose property they have confiscated; at the end of six months' imprisonment, he died most piously on the 3rd of the present month. On the 30th of November, the Feast of St Andrew, the tutelary saint of Scotland, one of our Fathers paid him a visit, and succeeded on the following night, with imminent danger to himself, to say mass, and administer the holy sacraments. There is no one for us but the good Jesus; yet, if He be for us, what matter who is against us? The only concern I have had during nearly the two last years is, that I remain alone in this southern part of the kingdom, and I have no one whose help I can procure for the good of my soul, and every hour I expect to be taken, or compelled to quit the country." [1]

But the tale becomes monotonous, and as we read the grim chronicle of the seventeenth century in Scotland the wonder grows that any vestige of the Faith survived. It is not until we realize the natural inclination of the predominatingly Celtic part of the country toward Catholicism that we begin

[1] Oliver: *Collections, S.J.* Quoted by Bellesheim.

III

to appreciate the fear of Popery's triumph which continuously haunted the Protestants of the south. It is no doubt true that the influence of the great house of Gordon was a dominant factor in preserving so comparatively large a slice of Aberdeen and Banff for Catholicism; but the steadfastness of the people under the pressure of over two centuries of either active persecution or at best of grinding disabilities must not be underestimated.

Take Braemar. When the storm of the Reformation burst, the priest of Braemar was John Owen, a holy man greatly loved by his parishoners. He stayed at his post, and with Almighty God's blessing upon his devotion his people held firmly to their faith. Owen was attacked at the altar by an armed band of ruffians and dragged off to prison in Aberdeen. On his way he told his assailants that the man who had struck him at the altar had thereby offended Almighty God, and prophesied that the arm which had struck him would rot and have to be amputated. The prophecy was fulfilled. In due course John Owen was released from prison and immediately returned to his parish, continuing to carry out his priestly duties in spite of the Protestant Terror. The poverty of the Church in the district of Braemar offered no temptation to the covetous, which no doubt helped to keep it out of the spoiler's eye.

After Father Owen's death the parish was served for many years by Jesuit missionaries and others who reached their flock in disguise. A Capuchin missionary, Father Epiphanius Lindsay, used to come, appropriately enough, dressed as a shepherd, and it was the sound of his flute upon the braes which summoned the faithful to their religious duties. We may take his career as typical of the times. Lindsay, who was a cadet of the house of Crawford, was educated in the Scots College at Louvain. After his ordination he returned to Scotland and worked in the south and south-west, reconciling many Protestants to the Church. He was arrested and condemned to death, but the sentence was commuted to perpetual banishment. In the Netherlands he was received into the Order of the Capuchins, and after a while made his way back to Scotland.

In a letter [1] to a brother Capuchin he writes:

"I came to Scotland," he says, "in 1620, only three priests being then known to me; and for ten years I exercised my ministry in the southern and western parts of the country. Then there sprang up a furious persecution of the Catholics. A nobleman, with the approval of the higher authorities, collected a force of three or four hundred horse and foot, invaded the

[1] Bellesheim: *History of the Catholic Church in Scotland*, Vol. IV, pp. 74, 75.

dwellings of the Catholics, seized their property, and threw them into prison. . . . He was succeeded by the preacher Ramsay, who became insane; then came John Brown, another preacher, who died a sudden death; next a viscount, who was carried off in ten days; and lastly a preacher named Gladmat (*sic*), who proved the most bitterly hostile of all to the Catholics. He burst into my house with an armed party, tore up books and vestments, seized the best things for himself, and had everything else publicly burnt. He proudly bragged of these deeds from the pulpit; but two months later he bit his tongue through with his teeth and gave up the ghost. Four years I spent here quite alone, without any companion. Three times I was betrayed, but never taken: the first informer denounced me to Lord Dunbar for a cloak and a hundred marks, the second to the preacher Thomas Renns, for a like sum. The preacher hunted through the whole house with his bailiffs, but did not find me, for I was concealed in the neighbouring wood. The third informer betrayed me to a Protestant kinsman; but being informed of the matter, I fled."

In spite of his disturbed existence, Father Epiphanius Lindsay lived to the age of eighty-four, not dying until four years after the Restoration. It sheds a sidelight on the inability of the Congregation of Propaganda to appreciate conditions in Scotland that in the Archives for 1647 there should be a note that the allowance to Father Epiphanius is reduced because of his failure to report on the state of his mission. There was a bureaucracy in Rome, on the whole more effective than most bureaucracies but not therefore less irritating.

The first resident priest at Braemar after the Reformation came there in 1671, and from that date until now the mission has never been vacant. Moreover, the population has not diminished as in so many other of the Catholic missions in the Highlands, not because the people turned from the religion of their fathers, but because they were driven from the land of their fathers by harsh economic circumstance. The evictions did not deliberately spare one creed more than any other, but the Catholic glens and islands suffered particularly because being always poverty-stricken and remote, they provided the excuse of expediency.

That in the diocese of Antigonish in Nova Scotia there should be over 80,000 Catholic Highlanders, more than half of whom are Gaelic-speaking, is a matter for imperial pride; but it does not compensate for the desolation of Glengarry and Knoydart, once a thickly populated Catholic district, now a wilderness with a congregation of hardly more than fifty souls. The emigration started as early as 1773 when a body of Catholic Gaels from Glengarry and Knoydart were largely instrumental in preserving Canada from the Colonies in revolt. Another five hundred went from Knoydart in 1786, and by 1850 successive emigrations had reduced the population of Knoydart to less than a thousand all told. A year later a brutal series of evictions occurred at the instance of the female owner of the Glengarry and Knoydart estates, on which by 1854 the Catholic inhabitants had been reduced to seventy.

The following excerpts from Mackenzie's *Highland Clearances* gives specific instances of mid-Victorian barbarism:

" Donald MacEachan, a cottar at Aror, married, with a wife and five children. This poor man, his wife and children, were fully twenty-three nights without any shelter but the broad and blue heavens. They kindled a fire and prepared their food beside a rock, and then slept in the open air. Just imagine the condition of this poor mother, Donald's wife, nursing a delicate child, and subjected to merciless storms of wind and rain during a long October night. One of the melancholy nights the blankets that covered them were frozen and white with frost.

" Alexander Macdonald, aged forty years, with a wife and family of four children, had his house pulled down. His wife was pregnant; still the levellers thrust her out, and then put the children out after her. The husband argued, remonstrated and protested, but it was all in vain; for in a few minutes all he had for his (to him comfortable) home was a lot of rubbish, blackened rafters, and heaps of stones. The levellers laughed at him and at his protests, and when their work was over moved away, leaving him to find refuge the best way he could. Alexander had, like the rest of his evicted brethren, to burrow among the rocks and caves until he put up a temporary shelter amid the wreck of his old habitation; but from this also he was repeatedly driven away. For three days Alexander Macdonald's wife lay sick beside a bush, where, owing to terror and exposure to cold, she had a miscarriage. She was then removed to the shelter of the walls of her former house, and for three days she lay so ill that her life was despaired of. These are facts as to which I challenge contradiction. I have not inserted them without the most satisfactory evidence of their accuracy.

" John Mackinnon, a cottar, aged forty-four, with a wife and six children, had his house pulled down and had no place to put his head; consequently he and his family, for the first night or two, had to burrow among the rocks near the shore! When he thought that the factor and his party had left the district, he emerged from the rocks, surveyed the ruins of his former dwelling, saw his furniture and other effects exposed to the elements, and now scarcely worth the lifting. The demolition was so complete that he considered it utterly impossible to make any use of the ruins of the old house. The ruins of an old chapel, however, were near at hand, and parts of the walls were still standing; thither Mackinnon proceeded with his family, and having swept away some rubbish and removed some grass and nettles, they placed a few cabers up to one of the walls, spread some sails and blankets across, brought in some meadow hay, and laid it in a corner for a bed, stuck a piece of iron into the wall in another corner, on which they placed a crook, then kindled a fire, washed some potatoes, put a pot on the fire and boiled them; and when these and a few fish roasted on the embers were ready, Mackinnon and his family had ONE good diet, being the first regular meal they tasted since the destruction of their house! Mackinnon's wife was pregnant when she was turned out of her house among the rocks. In about four days she had a premature birth; this and her exposure to the elements, together with the want of proper shelter and nutritious diet, has brought on consumption from which there is no chance whatever of her recovery.

" One would think that as Mackinnon took refuge amid the ruins of this most singular place, he would be left alone, and that he would not any longer be molested by man. But, alas, that was not to be! The manager of Knoydart and his minions arrived, and invaded this helpless family, even within the walls of the sanctuary. They pulled down the sticks and sails he had set up within its ruins—put his wife and children out on the cold shore—threw his tables, stools, chairs, etc., over the walls—burnt up the hay on which they slept—put out the fire—and then left the district. Four times have these officers broken in upon poor Mackinnon in this way, destroyed his place of shelter, and sent him and his family adrift on the cold coast of Knoydart. When I looked in upon these creatures last week I found them in utter consternation, having just learned that the officers would appear next day, and would again destroy the huts. The children looked at me as if I had been a wolf; they creeped behind their father, and stared wildly, dreading I was a law officer. The sight was most painful. The very idea that in Christian Scotland, and in the nineteenth century, these tender infants should be subjected to such gross treatment reflects strongly upon our humanity and civilization. Had they been suffering from the ravages of famine, or pestilence, or war, I could understand it and account for it, but suffering to gratify the ambition of some unfeeling speculator in brute beasts, I think it most unwarranted, and deserving the condemnation of every Christian man. Had Mackinnon been in arrears of rent, which he was not, even this would not justify the harsh, cruel and inhuman conduct pursued towards himself and his family. No language of mine can describe the condition of this poor family; exaggeration is impossible."

The Catholic Directory of 1855 announced:

" As the Catholics of this Mission have, with the exception of a mere handful, been evicted from their holdings and left to perish on the hill-side, or driven to seek in some foreign land, a shelter which was denied them in the land of their fathers, the Bishop has been compelled to withdraw the priest, and to attach what still remains of a venerable and flourishing Mission to North Morar. It is only five years since several hundred pounds were expended in building a commodious chapel and house in this district, neither of which is now of any use."

It may be repeated that equally atrocious treatment was often the lot of the Protestant crofters; but what must be emphasized is that the point of view which led to such treatment was the direct result of the Calvinistic interpretation of Christian doctrine, with its Judaic respect for material success as a sign of God's favour and the consequent subservience to externals like a Pharisaical Sabbath-worship at the expense of the reality of true holiness.

It is tempting to relate in detail the story of the Catholic missions on the mainland, of Strathglass and Lochaber and Badenoch, of Knoydart and Morar and Arisaig, of Glengarry, Glenmoriston, and Glencoe, and of many others; but space forbids. Something, however, must be said of the missionary work among the islands.

As early as the decade from 1610 to 1620, the General of the Jesuits was writing repeatedly to the Superior of the Jesuit Mission in Ireland, urging him to send missionaries to the Scottish Gaels; but it was left to some Irish Franciscan missionaries to make the first real effort in the Highlands and Islands.

In a report from Father John Brady to Propaganda in 1627, 10,000 conversions, or more accurately "reconciliations," were claimed in the Montana Scotiae, the term used in Rome for the Highlands and Islands. This was the Father Brady that was attacked by fourteen ministers, thrown from his horse, and severely wounded. In 1633 Father Patrick Hegarty was reporting that in the Hebrides he had reconciled 2229 souls to the Church, baptized 1222, and solemnized 117 marriages. The following year Propaganda was decreeing the restoration of the See of the Western Isles; but the proposal fell through.

At last, in 1651 when Clanranald sent from South Uist to Ireland to beg for more priests, Propaganda asked Saint Vincent de Paul, the founder of the Lazarists, for missionary help, and the Saint's response entitles him to be called the Apostle of the Hebrides. Father Francis White and Father Dermot Duggan, natives of Limerick and members of the Congregation of the Mission, were sent at once. They set out disguised as merchants, in the company of Young Glengarry, and they were in time to give the last Sacraments to Old Glengarry who was drawing near to a hundred years. Father White stayed in the Western Highlands; Father Duggan was assigned to the Islands; and Father Lumsden, a Scottish Lazarist, laboured in Orkney, Ross and Caithness, the only three priests by now in Montana Scotiae. On October 28th, 1652, Father Duggan was writing to Saint Vincent de Paul:

" I set out for the Hebrides, where God in His Omnipotent Mercy has worked wonders even beyond my hopes. He has so softened hearts there that Clanranald, Laird of a great part of Uist, has become a convert, together with his wife, his son and their whole family. This lead has been followed by all the gentry, the tenants and their families.

" MacNeill, Laird of the Island of Barra, having heard of me, sent a gentleman to beg me to do his island the same service as I had done for the Laird of Clanranald. . . . In these islands and in the whole of the Highlands of Scotland there are no priests except my companions and myself."

Eighteen months later he was writing:

" At the beginning of spring I landed upon another island, named Barra, where I found a people so devout and anxious to learn that I was astonished. It was enough to teach one child in each village the Pater, Ave and Credo; in two days the whole village knew them—children and adults. I have received all the leading inhabitants into the Church, including the young Laird with his brothers and sisters. There is hope of getting the old Laird on my next journey. Amongst the converts is a minister's son, whose devotion gives great edification throughout the whole district where he is known."

The labours of Father Duggan to establish the Faith in the Outer Islands lasted for five years, by the end of which time the people from Benbecula to Barra Head were safe under God against the basest ingenuity of man.

Throughout his apostolate Father Duggan was oppressed by the consciousness of the thousands of souls abandoned in the Isles from North Uist to Lewis.

On May 5th, 1657, he was writing:

" I am preparing to set out on the 10th of this month for Pabbay. I have not yet told you of this plan of mine fearing that the trouble and danger of it might make you anxious, for it really is a strange and weird place. Still, the hope we have of bringing back many stray sheep to the Lord's Fold, our trust in His goodness, and the grounds we have for hoping that the inhabitants of this island, not being infected with heresy, can, with God's grace, remain faithful to our religion if once instructed—those motives urge us to scorn the danger and even death and to set out with the help of God to Whose Will I submit myself."

Father Duggan was not granted the fulfilment of his purpose. On May 10th, 1657, he was in South Uist, preparing to set out on that mission, more dangerous than ever now when the rigours of Cromwellian thoroughness had reached as far as Lewis. He fell sick, and a week later he was dead.

However, his work endured. Dr Winster, the Prefect of the Scottish Missions, was able to write in a Report to the Sacred Congregation in 1669:

" The Catholics live in peace . . . in the islands of South Uist and Barra . . . which are the most remote from the government residences. Such is the severity of the laws that the practice of the Catholic religion is not allowed; in the Highlands, however, and remote islands these laws are not carried into execution. . . . The Highland families are, for the most part, Catholic or prepared to be so, if they had priests to instruct them; those, however, of the

Lowlands are most fierce heretics and hate the High-landers on account of their religion. The Highlanders are of excellent disposition, quick of intellect and taking a special delight in the pursuit of knowledge. They are desirous of novelties and have an abounded passion for ingenious inventions. No greater favour can be conferred on them than to educate their children and render them suited to become priests or ecclesiastics.

" Their untiring constancy in all matters is truly surprising and is admitted and extolled even by their enemies, particularly in regard of religion, which they continue to profess as much as the severity of the persecution and the total want of priests permit.

" Their arms are two-edged swords, large shields, bows and arrows, which they continue to use, adding to them, however, fire-arms, which they manage with admirable dexterity. . . . Almost all the families are Catholic or disposed to receive the Catholic Faith if for no other reason, at least to imitate their ancestors who were so zealous in the cause of religion.

" The remaining Scoto-Irish [1] are heretics more through ignorance than malice. They cease not, however, to cherish a great esteem for the Catholics, as appears in many things. If a priest visits them they show him more respect and honour him more than

[1] Note the hyphenation. We may hope that the present use of it for the Irish immigrants to the south of Scotland will in time become as obsolete as that earlier hyphenation.

their own ministers. In fact the heretics amongst the Highlanders surpass in reverence for our priests the very Catholics of the Lowlands. They moreover retain many Catholic usages, such as making the sign of the Cross, the invocation of Saints and sprinkling themselves with Holy Water, which they anxiously ask from their Catholic neighbours. In sickness they make pilgrimages to the ruins of the old churches and chapels which yet remain, as of the most noble monastery of Iona, where St Columba was Abbot: also of the chapels of Gairloch and Applecross and Glengarry which were once dedicated to the saints. They also visit the holy springs which yet retain the names of the saints to whom they were dedicated, and it has often pleased the Most High to restore to their health those who visited these ruins or drank at these springs invoking the aid of these saints.

" The enmity of the Lowlanders has been a great source of injury to the Scoto-Irish, especially since heresy began to dominate in Scotland, for the inhabitants of the Lowlands being most furious heretics (with the exception of some few whom the Catholic missionaries restored to the bosom of the Church), and seeing the Highlanders most constant in the Faith and that there is no hope of alienating them from the Church they seek by all possible means to excite odium against them, designating them as barbarians, impious enemies of the reformed creed, etc., and they hesitate not to affirm of them everything that can be suggested by detraction and their own excessive hatred. They even deem it a glorious deed to show contempt for or cast ridicule on a Highlander." [1]

By 1671 the Hebridean mission had been placed under the jurisdiction of Blessed Oliver Plunket, the martyred Archbishop of Armagh. Notwithstanding the tremendous task he had before him of trying to repair the devastation of Cromwell in Ireland the Archbishop contemplated a visitation of the Hebrides and even donning a belted plaid for the occasion. We obtain an interesting glimpse of current politics in the following extract from a letter:

" *Father Francis MacDonnell to Monsignor Baldeschi,
Secretary of Propaganda*

" ARMAGH, 10*th July* 1671.

" When I heard that His Grace the Primate of all Ireland had received from the Sacred Congregation the care of the Scottish Islands, or Hebrides, I hastened hither to Armagh from the Isles, in order that I might suggest how the Faith might be propagated in these Islands. His Grace himself greatly desired this summer to return there with me, but I was of the contrary

---

[1] The Whig historians and social theorists still circulate these old calumnies against the Gael.

opinion, inasmuch as a report had spread of the arrival of the French whom the Scots are said to favour, so that if His Grace, the Primate, were to go there, everyone would think that he had come to prepare the way for the French. It is for this same reason that no missionaries are to be sent there this summer, as the news of their arrival would at once get abroad and they would be cast into prison.

" For it is proposed to effect the union of the two kingdoms of England and Scotland in one Parliament, to which union the Islesmen are strongly opposed.

" Now, if the Primate were to visit them, it would at once be said that he came to foster the opposition to this union. The best and safest method of propagating the Catholic religion in the islands, and of strengthening it for the future, is to select some youths and to send them to Rome or to the seminaries on the Continent to be educated and promoted to the priesthood. Being natives, these may later do much good on the Isles and will be more gladly welcomed there. Meantime, His Grace the Primate should send thither some Irish priests or religious, since the people of these islands understand nothing but Gaelic, and they can hope for spiritual assistance from none but the Irish, since the Scots speak a corrupt form of English, and experience has long since proved that they afford no spiritual help to the Isles."

To this Report the Archbishop of Armagh added :

" The best method of propagating the Faith in these Islands is, first to send there missionaries knowing the Gaelic language, well grounded in virtue and inflamed with zeal for souls. The Procurator of the Mission, however, is of opinion that the Irish are scarcely fitted to minister there, inasmuch as there would be danger of the jealousy of the Royal Council, and if this were aroused the liberty now enjoyed would be lost. Hence it is necessary for many very important reasons to do everything as far as possible by means of priests of their own nation and to leave the jurisdiction over these people with those who are Scotch by nationality and that the Irish be there as their assistants."

This advice given by Blessed Oliver Plunket, with the substitution of other bodies for the Privy Council, is as pregnant to-day as when it was written.

In an attempt to deal with the problem of nurturing a native clergy, a school was founded on Barra in 1675. The only other Catholic school in Scotland was in Glengarry. Propaganda tried to insist that Catholic children should be sent to these schools from all the rest of Scotland, and Winster had to protest to the Cardinals that Catholic parents in Scotland would as soon send their children to school in Jamaica as in Barra.

In 1679 Father Alexander Leslie made a visitation

of the Scottish Vicariate. He reported to Propaganda that there were 12,000 Catholics in the Highlands and Islands with four priests, three of whom were Irish and the fourth, Father Robert Munro, the first native Gaelic speaker ordained since the Reformation, with whom he sailed to the Islands.

Father Munro was a devoted priest. Between 1671 and 1704 he was often imprisoned and twice banished from the country. In 1696 he was arrested in Flanders and charged with " rebellion " against Dutch William. On his release he returned to Scotland, became acting Dean of the Isles, and in the winter of 1704 was arrested yet again and imprisoned in one of the dungeons of Glengarry Castle, without a wisp of straw for a bed or so much as a glass of water to cool the fever from which he was suffering. In two days he was dead. It was a black time.

" Men," wrote Chambers in his *Domestic Annals*,[1] " in trying to make each other Episcopalians and Presbyterians, had almost ceased to be Christians. The population was small and generally poor, and little had been done to advance the arts of life. Scotland had sent forth no voice in either literature or science; her universities could not train either the lawyer or the physician. No news-sheet, no stage-coaches, no system of police, existed in the realm. In

[1] Vol. II, p. 497.

certain intellectual and moral respects, the country was in no better state. The judge was understood to be accessible to private persuasions, and even direct bribes were suspected. The people believed as firmly in witchcraft as in the first principles of religion."

But Chambers was a bit of a Jacobite, and a quotation from Lecky,[1] the rationalist historian, will be less suspected of a bias in favour of Catholicism :

" There was one country in which the Puritan ministers succeeded in moulding alike the character and the habits of the nation, and in disseminating their harsh and gloomy tenets through every section of society. While England was breaking loose from her most ancient superstitions and advancing with gigantic strides along the paths of knowledge, Scotland still cowered in helpless subjection before her clergy. Never was a tyranny maintained with more inexorable barbarity. Supported by public opinion, the Scottish ministers succeeded in overawing all opposition, and prohibiting the faintest expression of adverse opinions."

This state of affairs was the aftermath of what a modern Scottish historian [2] calls " a militant Scottish imperialism . . . as superior to the ambitious projects of other nations, before and since, as it was inferior to them in practical common sense."

[1] Lecky : *History of Rationalism*, Vol. I, pp. 137–8.
[2] Colin Walkinshaw : *A Scots Tragedy*, pp. 113, 114.

" But the fact that the dream was impossible," the writer continues, " should not blind us to its quality. It is true that in this case the unity of the national effort was less than it had been in the days of Wallace and Bruce. The Highlands, the relics of the old Gaelic Scotland, were now almost completely cut off in spirit and civilization from the determining mass of the country. . . . The revolution in religion which had been remaking Lowland Scotland had scarcely penetrated the remoter glens and the isles, so that great regions were left almost without a church. . . . And now the Highlanders were to take their revenge by hamstringing the nation in its supreme crisis."

And what was this dream of quality? It was a dream to force upon England that particular religious system whose triumphs had already reduced Scotland to a condition of moral and spiritual degradation that can only be paralleled by the Germany of the Thirty Years War. It was a dream to demonstrate by force of arms the conviction of two-thirds of the Scottish nation that the Scots had succeeded the Jews as the Chosen People. It was a dream that inspired the Scots to sell their King to the English for the pay owing to them for fighting with such grand mercenary fervour on behalf of the same dream. And even that traitors' bargain was a bad business, for of course the English never did pay those sordid fanatics who sold their King, and whose descendants, sixty years later, would sell their country to the same bidder. It should be no matter for regret, but a healing balm to the national pride that Montrose and his Gaels did hamstring such a part of a nation.

Yet it was not the Gaels who finally dissipated that dream of quality. That was left for fellow-dreamers, at the tragic farce of Dunbar fight. It was September again, the month of Flodden and Pinkie Cleugh. The English army under Cromwell consisted chiefly of the sect known as Independents, which permitted all its votaries to be preachers. On the other hand the divine rage of the Presbyterians prompted their ministers to assume the authority of officers, which from a military standpoint was a more dangerous eccentricity.

When Cromwell invaded Scotland early in the summer of 1650 he was out-generalled for some time by Leslie until at last he actually found himself in a position of considerable peril, with the Scots occupying an impregnable position and himself and his troops faced with the necessity of a hazardous retreat. Leslie had only to wait; but the Presbyterian ministers, crazed by their Israelitish obsession, demanded that their army should go down against the Philistines at Gilgal, or in ordinary language abandon their strong position and attack the English on the level. Cromwell, who was just as much convinced of his Israelitish status as the Scots, discerned in this manœuvre an assurance that God had delivered his enemies into his hand. The officers of both sides were ranting away. The sun rose out of the Firth of Forth. " Let the Lord arise, and let His enemies be scattered," Cromwell observed. The two Chosen Peoples engaged, but the English veterans of the holy war against the Malignants were too good for the raw levies of the Covenant. The Scots were defeated with heavy slaughter, and the many Scottish prisoners were sold as slaves on the English settlements in America.

Spiritual pride has rarely had such an ignominious fall.

The final humiliation came three years later. When the General Assembly of 1653, meeting at Edinburgh, was about to begin its business, an English officer, Colonel Cotterel came in to demand whether the Assembly sat by authority of Parliament, of the Commander-in-Chief, or of the English judges. Without waiting for the Moderator to reply, Cotterel dissolved the Assembly, and had the members led out of Edinburgh under military escort.

The Presbyterians, cheated of their imperial theocracy, turned to witch-hunting to show their zeal for God's Word. Not the least painful wound that the history of that ghastly century inflicts upon a Scotsman's pride is the discovery that the English judges appointed by Cromwell did their best to stop the witch-hunts and earned in consequence the reputation of being themselves minions of Satan. Only in the Highlands and Islands where the Catholic Faith, in spite of persecution, in spite of penal laws, in spite of the rarity of their poverty-stricken harried priests, shed the light that attends spiritual progress, were old women safe from being burnt alive, sometimes at the instigation of the ecclesiastic authorities, sometimes at the demand of the ignorant mob.

CHAPTER VII

NOTWITHSTANDING the triumphant success of the Catholic missionaries to the Islands, it would be correct to say that during the second half of the seventeenth century the future of the Faith in Scotland never looked so hopeless. The steady economic persecution of a hundred years had been the deciding factor. Presbyterians and Episcopalians had between them almost succeeded in literally starving out their opponents. It was small wonder that the secular priests were tempted sometimes to allow their converts to continue attandance at heretical services in order to avoid the financial ruin which followed excommunication by the Kirk. This caused scandal to the older Catholics who had held out at all costs against even an expedient pretence of conforming to the tyrannous religious system enjoying political power.

Space is lacking to discuss here the internal difficulties of the Scottish mission at this melancholy time; but the Catholic reader will find much valuable information gathered together by Major M. V. Hay in *The Blairs Papers* 1603–1660, and when he has studied that scholarly work he will be more completely assured than ever of the impotency of the gates of Hell to prevail against the Church of which by God's mercy he is a member. And the most superficial perusal of a book like that might suggest to the bewildered Protestant of to-day why Catholics are able to regard with such comparative equanimity the general attack upon the Christian Faith now proceeding all along the line.

There was a brief lull in the persecution on the accession to the throne of James VII and II, of all Scottish or English monarchs the most unjustly maligned. It is significant that in his two edicts of toleration proclaimed in 1686 James gave a solemn promise that those who held Church property should be confirmed in their possession of it. Having overcome thereby, as he might suppose, the most vital objection to toleration for Catholics, he proceeded to suspend the penal statutes against them, to declare himself in favour of liberty of conscience for all religious denominations, and to promise to uphold the rights of the Established Kirk.

Two years later James was driven from his throne, and armed mobs in Edinburgh, inflamed by the Presbyterian ministers, murdered the guard in Holyrood, sacked the chapel and library, and burnt the houses of many Catholics.

The reign of the Dutchman William was marked in Scotland by an extension of penal legislation against Catholics varied by such incidents as the massacre of the Catholic Macdonalds of Glencoe and the torture of the unfortunate Englishman Payne, on William's personal warrant, to extract details of an alleged plot to restore King James. In May 1700 the Scottish Parliament passed an Act authorizing a reward of 500 merks for the detection of priests, and the immediate banishment of such from the country on pain of death if they returned. By the same Act Catholics were formally debarred from educating their own children and declared incapable of inheriting property.

The increasing dangers and difficulties of the Scottish mission had at last made an impression on the Congregation of Propaganda, which in 1694 decided to nominate a vicar-apostolic for Scotland with episcopal consecration. The choice fell upon Thomas Nicolson, who at this date was fifty-five years of age.

"He had been brought up a Protestant and for fourteen years was a professor at Glasgow University. He had become a Catholic in 1682 and was ordained priest in 1685. He had been working on the Scottish mission when the Revolution started in 1688. Escaping from Edinburgh he was imprisoned in Stirling, but after some months allowed to leave the country. In

1695 he was nominated Vicar-Apostolic and consecrated as Bishop of Peristachium. For a year he was kept in Holland, and when at last William gave him a licence to enter England, on his way to his duties he was nevertheless arrested on landing and kept in prison for some months.

"His first report to Rome was sent from Aberdeen in September 1697. He gave a good account of the learning, zeal, and holiness of the scattered missionaries, but was much grieved by the harm done to Catholics by the growing infidelity and the general corruption of morals."

In the early summer of 1700 Bishop Nicolson held his first visitation of the Highlands and Islands. On Eigg he found the whole population Catholic—three hundred in number and "very constant in the faith." An English pirate called Porringer had landed there a few years previously and tried to make them renounce their church at the point of the knife. From Canna, with a hundred and thirty Catholics, the Bishop crossed over to South Uist and Benbecula to find fifteen hundred Catholics, nine hundred of whom he confirmed. From South Uist the Bishop visited Barra where he would have found at least another thousand. At the end of July he visited Arisaig and other districts on the western mainland, confirming no less than three thousand persons. In his report to Rome the

Bishop stressed the importance of providing Gaelic-speaking mission priests and noted that the compulsory Protestant education of the sons of the chieftains had been responsible for the loss of many Catholics. He gave as an instance the apostasy of the Maclean chief, who however had returned to the faith and was now in exile with King James. Not so, however, his clan, who had followed him into Protestantism, but without returning. At the end of his report Bishop Nicolson pointed out that the Protestant education of the chieftains' sons meant that their dependants and friends in taking advantage of their learning imbibed heresy with it, there not being enough priests to counter this influence. For this the Bishop blamed, somewhat bitterly, the fathers of the Society of Jesus whom he accused of trying to keep the Scottish mission a close preserve for the Society, "themselves remaining in the houses of Catholic nobles without troubling themselves at all about the Highlands."

The death of William brought no relief. The ministers, having overthrown their enemies the Episcopalian clergy, now had more time to concentrate upon the elimination of the Catholics. In Edinburgh, on the eve of the opening of the General Assembly of 1703, the common hangman and his assistants dressed up in vestments pillaged from Catholic houses, with crucifixes and chalices in their vile hands, paraded the streets at the head of a mob yelling blasphemous execrations. Queen Anne a month or two later issued a proclamation calling on all sheriffs, bailies, magistrates, etc., to put the laws against Papists into vigorous motion and exhorting the ministers to be diligent in finding out all persons suspected of Popery. The lists of Catholics reported to the Commission of the General Assembly from 1701 to 1705 show a hundred and sixty Catholics from Edinburgh, five from Leith, twelve from Glasgow, and twenty from Perth. The Synod of Dumfries complained that the Papists there had stuck a sword in the minister's horse in revenge for his getting their priest Father Innes arrested.

A report from the Highlands and Islands must have been gloomy reading for the Established Kirk. " First—South Uist and Barra : the people here are nearly all Papists. Second—Canna, Rum, and Muck : all Popish. Third—Knoydart and Morar : all Papists except four. Fourth—Arisaig, Moydart, and Glengarry : all Papists except one man. . . . There are six priests and only five ministers in the whole bounds of the Presbytery of Skye." From the north the " minister of the united parishes of Glenmuick, Tullich and Glengarden " sent a report in 1704 that " Calam Griersone, *alias* McGregor, of Ballater " had

" leatly . . . erected a very high crucifix on a little hill near his house, to be adored by all the neighbourhood. He always keeps publick Mass and popish conventicles in his house and is such a trefecter that fiew or no Protestants that become his tenants, or servants, excape without being preverted by him." This stout fellow was also accused of mimicking the minister's preaching !

In 1707 the political metamorphosis of Scotland into North Britain was effected by the Act of Union which brought to a shameful conclusion that long transaction which was first made a practical possibility by the Reformers when they sacrificed their country on the altar of religious hate.

Care was taken by the terms of the " Treaty " for the maintenance and establishment of Presbyterianism. Neither liberty of worship, nor even liberty of conscience, was granted to those Scots whose faith was the faith of Wallace and Bruce.

The Rising of 1715 brought fresh miseries for the Catholics ; but the growth of Catholicism in the insurgent north and west remained a source of despair to the Protestants. " The great matter we have before us," wrote Wodrow from the General Assembly in 1721, " is the terrible growth of Popery in the north. . . . The accounts are most lamentable. . . . Bishops, priests, and Jesuits are exercising openly their functions, seminaries and schools are openly set up, and multitudes sent abroad and coming home from Popish seminaries every three or four months." [1]

Note the word "multitudes." It is typical of Protestant exaggeration in pamphlet or pulpit.

In 1725 George I subscribed £1000 to the funds of the Church of Scotland for providing catechists to work at "converting" the Catholic Highlands. This was doubled by George IV, is known as the "royal bounty," and is still paid. At the same time the Society for the Propagating of Christian Knowledge under the guise of philanthropic education was working hard to deprive the unfortunate Catholics in the Western Highlands of their ancient faith. With bitterness it has to be recorded that the custom, widely spread during the eighteenth and nineteenth centuries, of trying to buy Catholics into Protestantism was initiated by the Society for the Propagating of Christian Knowledge.

In 1728 Scottish Catholics suffered a grievous loss by the death of their lay leader, the second Duke of Gordon, for his widow, an English Protestant, after a solemn death-bed promise that she would keep the children faithful to the religion of their father, brought them up in her own religion, for which she was rewarded with a Government pension of £1000.

[1] Wodrow : *Correspondence*, Vol. II, p. 586.

One of her grandsons was the lunatic Lord George Gordon, that distinguished champion of No Popery who at last discovered that the logical conclusion of No Popery was to grow a long beard and become a Jew, in which religion he lived to the end of a worthless and mischievous life.

Bishop Nicolson, who in 1712 had founded the seminary of Scalan among the remote braes of Glenlivet, had died in 1718, worn out by the anxieties of the '15. He was succeeded by Bishop Gordon with Bishop Wallace for coadjutor. Some extracts from a report [1] of theirs to Propaganda dated July 4th, 1730, gives a vivid picture of the current state of affairs :

" Although no general persecution has raged here against the faithful, yet in certain districts, owing to the cruel instigation of the preachers, they have been very severely treated by the authorities. In the Island of Mull, for example, out of several respectable persons who had embraced the Catholic faith, one, who was the best known, has been thrown into prison, another has been forced to leave the kingdom, while others have had to quit that part of the country, and have hardly been able to find a living anywhere else. In most of the districts where Catholics are comparatively numerous, the ministers annoy them in a thousand ways, lay snares to catch them, and in the

[1] Translated by Bellesheim and printed in the appendix to Vol. IV.

case of poor persons especially, when they will not conform to their wishes, get the magistrates to harass and fine them.

"We suffer under various other troubles, for on the one hand the ministers are multiplied, together with their catechists and schoolmasters, especially in those places where Catholics abound, are often thrust upon an unwilling people, and when they can, and dare, under the protection of the local landowners, drag into their temples, even by employing force, farmers, artificers, and other poorer Catholics, beating and driving them with clubs when they make vigorous resistance. On the other hand, the number of missionaries diminishes, and will further diminish, some of them abandoning us on account of the want which they suffer here, others with their strength exhausted, and labouring under infirmities and diseases; while many others again threaten every day to quit the mission, since we are unable to supply them even with a tolerable subsistence. . . . There are very many heretics who aspire to the faith and implore our help, often entreating in tearful accents that Catholic priests may be stationed among them, and promising that if they are not abandoned by them they will profess the faith with great readiness and constancy. We cannot without much grief listen to men of this kind, so piously inclined towards the faith, and we grieve for them the more bitterly, inasmuch as in very many cases we have had good proof of their sincerity. . . . There is now above all an urgent need, as we have more than once pointed out to your Eminences, of appointing a bishop for the Highland district; for it is in that quarter that there is the greatest danger from the preachers, since there especially heretical ministers and pernicious schools are increasing; and in that region especially there are many places in which there is excellent hope of gaining large numbers of souls, if we had the means of stationing several missionaries among them."

The appeal for a Highland bishop was granted by the nomination of Hugh Macdonald, a son of the laird of Morar, who had been educated at Scalan. In 1731 he was consecrated Bishop of Diana *in partibus* and formally appointed first Vicar-Apostolic to the Highlands and Islands.

In 1732, Bishop Macdonald was writing to Propaganda:

" In the place of certain deceased priests, necessity has compelled the appointment of others from districts further south; and these, although of Highland family, want of practice has rendered almost useless at our mountain language, which they lost when studying at the colleges abroad. The faithful grievously deplore this scarcity of pastors, and while others enjoy in abundance every convenience for their spiritual welfare, they constantly complain that their souls are starving, by reason, not of the negligence, but of the fewness, of labourers in the vineyard. A great number of the heretics lament, in presence of the bishop or priest, with groans, tears, and words that might move stones, over their own unhappy errors and blindness; and having at length discovered the impiety, avarice, and carelessness of their ministers, and had their eyes opened to certain enormous errors, implore the help of Holy Mother Church, and ask with continual and unspeakable eagerness for Catholic pastors. Hence the greatest sorrow is enkindled in my heart, seeing as I do that the number of labourers amongst us who are versed in the Highland tongue is so scanty, that they are not only insufficient to assist Protestants of the kind I have described, but even the very Catholics themselves."

It was Bishop Macdonald who, as he was crossing Loch Lochy, on his way back from a conference at Edinburgh with the vicar-apostolic for the Lowlands, heard the news of the landing of Prince Charles Edward. With his long and harsh experience of what such an enterprise might mean to the Catholic Gaels the Bishop urged the Prince to abandon his attempt; but when he saw the spontaneous enthusiasm of the Catholic clans for one who seemed to them the liberator for whom they had been waiting ever since the brief reign of James VII had given them a taste and a promise of economic and political freedom, the Bishop no longer demurred. He blessed the royal banner at Glenfinnan, and allowed his priests to march as chaplains with the Prince's army.

In spite of the unanimity with which the Catholics of Scotland yearned for the successful issue of that enterprise it would be a most unwarrantable pretension to claim that the Rising of 1745 was a Catholic rising, or indeed a specifically religious demonstration in any way. The large majority of the Prince's followers consisted of Catholics and Episcopalians, but there was a considerable number of Presbyterians who defied the wild denunciations of their ministers and joined him. No doubt the ministers were wise to oppose the Prince's attempt, for although his success would have brought nothing more to Catholics than another edict of toleration like those of his grandfather James VII, toleration in the middle of the eighteenth century would have meant that within ten years the whole of Gaelic Scotland would have been reconciled to the Catholic Church. Nobody who has discovered from a book like Sage's *Memorabilia Domestica* what the religious condition of Ross-shire and Sutherland was during the second half of the eighteenth century will dispute such an assertion. To the Gaelic districts would have been added a great extension of Catholic influence from the staunch heart of Aberdeenshire and Banffshire, and if we may judge by the *rapprochement* between the Catholic and Episcopalian Jacobites, which went so far as hearing Mass together on several occasions during the march south, it is not trespassing into excessive speculation to suggest that the whole Episcopalian body in Scotland might have submitted to the Church within a comparatively short time, and thus avoided the impasse in which it now exists, an anomalous body of Catholic-minded Christians incapable of taking spiritual advantage of the rapid decay of Presbyterianism as a vital religious force. More was lost at Culloden than an earthly kingdom.

The revenge taken by the British Government was further sweetened by the excuse rebellion afforded to proceed with the utmost rigour against the Catholic laity and the Catholic clergy. Chapels were destroyed; the seminary at Scalan was burnt: vestments and missals made a hangman's bonfire: transportations and executions continued for months. As late as 1755 Bishop Macdonald, who had returned to Scotland in 1749 after a withdrawing to the continent with other Jacobites implicated in the Rising, was arrested and sentenced to banishment for life. Nevertheless, he remained in the Highlands as Bishop until his death in 1773.

Before the '45 there had been dissensions among the priests of the Scottish mission, due partly to resentment of Jesuit influence, partly to the spread of Jansenism, which was rife in the Scots College in Paris. It is strange that in a country of individualists like Scotland any doctrinal school which has impugned man's free will has always been secure of a ready following. Yet it is easy to understand that the constancy and fervour of priests and people alike were suffering from a temporary exhaustion after the stupendous fortitude which had battled for Christ's Church through nearly two centuries in a country more utterly abandoned than any in the world to the sheer lust of religious hate. England in the middle of the eighteenth century from a utilitarian point of view had justified to the very last drop of Catholic blood her establishment of a special religion for Englishmen. Insular and insolent, Britannia could afford to despise the rest of Europe. But Scotland? Scotland for the rest of Europe was now a province, hardly a province indeed, but a mere bleak prolongation of England. So a cheated nation dreamed of possessions in the next world, dreamed of a paradise reserved for His favourites by Almighty God, a paradise as spacious and empty as a deer-forest, from which even the richest Englishmen would be excluded. Secure in this belief, the Elect delighted to give

Papists a foretaste on earth of that hell in which they were doomed to burn eternally. For such behaviour they fancied they found Divine encouragement in that Old Testament which at the caprice of private citation had become the sole test of their morality.

This fury of sectarian hate, which still rages more fiercely in Scotland than anywhere else on earth, was never allowed to cool. We who are aware of the ignorant lies about Catholics and Catholicism which are given currency even to-day by too many Protestants have to imagine what the effect of trying to fight against those lies year after year must have been upon a poverty-stricken small minority. Exhaustion was inevitable. Yet, at the very moment when the fortunes of the Catholic mission were at their lowest ebb and when at last it was seeming to the eager ministers that within a few more years Scotland would be finally " purged of Popery," the right man by God's mercy was granted to His stricken Church in Scotland.

When the Prince, solicitous for the wounded after Prestonpans, sent into Edinburgh for surgeons George Hay, an Episcopalian medical student just turned sixteen, was one of those who answered his appeal. He accompanied the Prince's army on the march to Derby, but during the retreat was seized with an ague and had to return to Edinburgh. He was arrested and sent down to London as a prisoner. Here he fell in with a Catholic bookseller called Meighan who lived in Drury Lane, and after this opportunity to read books and discuss the truth he returned to Scotland as soon as the Act of Indemnity made it possible. In December 1748 Hay was received into the Church by Father Seton, S.J. He then resumed his medical studies, only to discover that the penal laws made it impossible for him as a Catholic to become a doctor of medicine. For a while he kept a chemist's shop in Edinburgh, but later he obtained a job as a surgeon on a merchant ship sailing from London. Here he met Bishop Challoner, the Vicar-Apostolic of the London district, who being much impressed by the young surgeon's abilities and natural piety urged him to test his vocation for the priesthood. Hay left his ship at Marseilles and entered the Scots College in Rome, where after eight years of study he was ordained priest in 1758.

By a coincidence his first mission was Rathven where an ancestor of the same name had been priest at the Reformation and apostatized, afterwards achieving some renown as a Protestant controversialist. Ten years later at the age of thirty-nine Hay was consecrated at Scalan Bishop of Daulis *in partibus* as coadjutor of Bishop Grant, on whose death in 1778 he became Vicar-Apostolic of the Lowlands.

In 1770 soon after Bishop Hay's consecration Macdonald of Boisdale launched an odious persecution against the people of South Uist. He began with the children by driving them to Protestant schools where they were compelled to copy out scurrilous sentences and during Lent had flesh-meat forced into their mouths. When the parents withdrew their children, Boisdale assembled his tenants and ordered them either to renounce Catholicism or lose their holdings. The poor people replied that they would rather beg from door to door than forsake their faith. Boisdale had already driven Father Wynne the priest from the island with threats of personal violence, and he now offered to leave the people in possession of their land if they would let the children be brought up as Protestants. To this the parents replied that the souls of the little ones were as dear to them as their own. Boisdale then proceeded to carry out his threat of wholesale eviction. Bishop Hay published a memorial setting forth the case of the poor Uist people and raised subscriptions to meet the cost of transporting them to America in 1772.

The walls of Boisdale's garden are still to be seen, dry and grey as the ribs of a dead whale, but the great house he built himself has been pulled down to provide stone for byres. His line is extinct. On his death-bed he cried out in agony of mind for a priest, but the sons he had brought up as Protestants refused his last request, and he died with remorse and terror heavy upon his soul.

In 1777 a Bill to relieve English Catholics of some of their disabilities came before Parliament, and perhaps it was the hope that this relief might be extended to Scottish Catholics which led Bishop Hay to propose that George III should be prayed for by name. Until then the King prayed for had always been intended to be the rightful king. No doubt the refusal of the Pope to acknowledge the Count of Albany as a reigning monarch influenced Bishop Hay. His proposal was accepted without much opposition from the clergy, and from that time onwards the Sovereigns of the Protestant Succession have been publicly prayed for in all Catholic churches in Scotland.

The idea of relieving Catholics of any of their disabilities seized the Presbyterians with apprehensive fury. The General Assembly of 1778 protested against the Bill, and some months later the Synod of Glasgow and Ayr appointed a general fast-day on account of the "awful signs of divine displeasure which are visibly displayed at this time, particularly the encouragement given to and the growth of Popery. The astonishing progress of this detestable, cruel, and unjust superstition, is so much the more alarming, as it appears not only in remote and uncultivated corners, but in the most populous and improved parts of the land."

The following is an abstract of the penal laws against Catholics, the slightest relief of which was believed by the Protestants to be a sign of Almighty God's irritation. It is quoted by Bellesheim from Lord Kames's *Statute Law* (*abridged*).

" All professors of the Catholic religion were obliged to quit the country, unless they would subscribe the Confession of Faith. The purchase or dissemination of the Catholic books were punishable with banishment and confiscation of personal property. Jesuits and seminary priests were to be pursued, apprehended, and punished with death and confiscation. The harbouring or entertainment of them was likewise punishable with confiscation. Those guilty of hearing mass, of refusing to attend the Protestant service, or of endeavouring to pervert any of His Majesty's subjects, either by reasoning or by books, were liable to be searched out and destroyed by the magistrates, and importers of such books to be committed to prison during the king's pleasure. The presbyteries were authorized to summon before them ' all Papists, and those suspected of Papistry,' and to require them to make satisfaction to the Kirk: failing which they were to be denounced to the Privy Council, and their property escheated to the Crown; and all persons harbouring them were likewise liable to confiscation. Anyone suspected of being a Jesuit, priest, or ' trafficking Papist,' and convicted of changing his name or surname, incurred sentence of perpetual banishment, under pain of death if he returned to Scotland; and a similar penalty was incurred by mere presence at any meeting ' where there is altar, mass-book, vestments, Popish images, or other Popish trinkets.' Heavy fines were imposed on noblemen or others sending their sons to be educated in foreign seminaries; and parents whose children became Catholics abroad had to find caution that they would send them no pecuniary assistance, except for the purpose of bringing them back to Scotland. Children under the care of Catholic parents or guardians were to be taken from them, and intrusted to some ' well-affected and religious friend,' the means for their support and education being provided out of the property of their parents. Severe penalties were incurred for the crime of converting to the Catholic faith any of His Majesty's Protestant subjects; and a Protestant servant becoming a Catholic was punished as an apostate, and was forbidden to take a situation in any Catholic family. Catholics were incapable of acquiring real property, either by purchase or by deed of gift made in their favour, or in trust on their behalf, such deeds being by law absolutely null and void. They were also incapable, after the age of fifteen, of inheriting estates: if the heir, on attaining that age, refused to renounce his faith, his right of succession lapsed, passing to the nearest Protestant heir. If the latter declined to avail himself of it, it passed to the next Protestant after him, and so on until as worded in the statute the right was 'effectually established' in the Protestant line. All dispositions, donations, and legacies in favour of ' cloisters, or other Popish societies,' were *ipso facto* null and void; nor were Catholics permitted to make any disposition of their property in prejudice of their heirs-apparent. A Protestant turning Catholic forfeited his whole heritable estate to his nearest Protestant heir. No Catholic could be king or queen of the realm, ' or bear any office whatever therein '; and not only Catholics, but persons marrying Catholics, were incapable of ever succeeding to the crown. Catholics could be neither governors, schoolmasters, guardians, nor factors, a fine of a thousand merks being imposed on those who employed them in such capacities. They were forbidden to teach 'any art, science, or exercise of any sort,' under a penalty of five hundred merks. Protestants were prohibited from employing Catholic servants, under the same penalty; and the informer in such cases was entitled to the amount of the fine as his reward."

On the Sunday after that expression of Christian charity from the Glasgow Synod previously quoted, a mob attacked and destroyed the only Catholic chapel in Glasgow, which was in a private house in the old Saltmarket, the worshippers being pelted with stones and refuse. A Mr Bagnall, an Englishman resident in Glasgow, now offered his house for divine service, but an association called 'The Friends to Protestantism' organized another riot which ended in the burning of Mr Bagnall's home and warehouses. Lest contemporary Edinburgh should be jealous of this display of Christian fervour let us quickly add that the riots in the capital were equally violent. A circular signed "A Protestant" was broadcast in Edinburgh. "Whoever shall find this letter, will take as a warning to meet at Leith Wynd, on Wednesday next in the evening, to pull down that pillar of Popery lately erected there." On the feast of the Purification the chapel-house was duly attacked. The mob forced its way in with hammers, and within a short time the house was fired. Many other Catholic houses were wrecked, while the city fathers who had taken no steps to avert the riot did nothing to suppress it.

It is pleasant to be able to quote the courageous speech that Principal Robertson made before the General Assembly in 1779 :

"My character as a man, as a citizen, and as a

minister of the Gospel has been delineated in the most odious colours : I have been represented as a pensioner of the Pope, as an agent for Rome, as a seducer of my brethren to Popery, as the tool of a king and ministry bent on overturning the Protestant religion. In pamphlets, in newspapers, and hand-bills, I have been held out to an enraged mob as the victim who deserved to be next sacrificed, after they had satiated their vengeance on a Popish bishop. . . . For several weeks hardly a day passed on which I did not receive incendiary letters, several of them signed by 'Lovers of Truth' and 'Friends to the Protestant Religion.' It was in the name of Jesus I was warned that my death was resolved, and the instruments prepared for cutting short my days. May God forgive the men who have disseminated such principles."

Catholics will remember with equal admiration the courageous rebuke administered to the Protestant *canaille* of modern Edinburgh by Principal Macgregor in the Church of Scotland magazine, *Life and Work*.

In that month of February 1779, Bishop Hay addressed a pastoral letter, from which we may extract a few sentences :

". . . Above all things, we enjoin you not to allow the smallest resentment to enter your hearts against those who injure us : remember they are only the instruments in the hands of God, who, like a tender father, chastises us His children by their means, but who could not touch a hair of our heads except in as far as they are permitted by Him. In this view, let us have all compassion towards them, and pity their mistaken zeal, which makes them think that by persecuting us they do God a service. Let us imitate the example which our Lord gives us on the cross, and pray for them in His words, ' Father, forgive them ; for they know not what they do.' "

Attempts were made in Parliament by John Wilkes and Edmund Burke to obtain as much relief for Scottish Catholics as had already been granted to English Catholics. It was no use. The Scottish members were ruled by fear of the Edinburgh mob. Next year London was to experience the Gordon Riots, of which Gibbon wrote, " The month of June 1780 will ever be marked by a dark and diabolical fanaticism which I supposed to be extinct, but which actually subsists in Great Britain perhaps beyond any country in Europe."

It was not until 1793 that the Lord Advocate ventured to introduce a Bill to relieve some of the disabilities of Scottish Catholics. They were now allowed the peaceful possession and free disposition of their property ; but they were still excluded from almost every office and profession, and they were still compelled to be married by the parish minister and pay baptismal dues to the parish officials.

The strain of the Napoleonic Wars following upon the political anxieties created by the French Revolution preoccupied the public mind sufficiently to give the Catholic bogey a rest. At the beginning of the nineteenth century Bishop Hay was able to report that the thirty thousand faithful could worship freely in their twelve churches served by three bishops and forty priests, all natives of Scotland. In the year 1811 Bishop Hay died at the age of eighty-three. He had cherished his flock as a wise and devoted bishop for nearly forty-four years, and the Church in Scotland owes him an inestimable debt.

During the first quarter of the nineteenth century the desire of the godly Presbyterian employers for cheap labour reduced them to take advantage of the wretched condition of an Ireland oppressed by English misrule to encourage a huge flow of Irish immigration, and although at the same time hundreds of Catholic Highlanders were being driven across the Atlantic by the tyranny of Protestant landlords the Catholic population increased at a rapid pace. In Edinburgh and Leith their numbers went up from a thousand in 1800 to over 14,000 in 1829, and in Glasgow there were 25,000 Catholics in that year.

Efforts to secure complete emancipation for Catholics

had begun with a Bill proposed by Fox in 1805, but almost another quarter of a century was to pass before such a Bill became law. As the prospect of this drew nearer the Presbyterians worked hard to prevent the passage of the Bill, organizing monster petitions and indignation meetings all over the country. Fortunately for Scotland and English Catholics, the Irish led by Daniel O'Connell had succeeded in frightening even Wellington with the prospect of a state of turbulence in Ireland at a time of considerable social unrest in England. On March 13th, Peel carried the Third Reading of the Bill through the House of Commons, and a month later Wellington overcame the prejudice of the Lords. George IV declared he would rather have his head cut off than give the Royal assent; but after drinking immense potations of cherry brandy, that King, of whom Greville said that " a more contemptible, cowardly, unfeeling, selfish dog did not exist," surrendered and signed. A few minor disabilities were retained; with the progress of time those too have disappeared.

The first fruit of emancipation was the foundation of Blairs College to take the place of the small seminaries of Lismore and Aquhorties. Presently the devotion of the Catholic clergy during the cholera outbreak of 1832 so much impressed the people of Edinburgh, that there was little opposition when an

Ursuline convent, the first nuns since the Reformation, was founded in the capital.

The next step forward on which Scottish Catholics concentrated their hopes was the restoration of the hierarchy. The difficulties of the vicariates had been aggravated by the *imperium in imperio* which the Irish immigrants, fervently supported by their parish priests, tried to set up. During the sixties the ill-feeling between the Irish and the Scots reached an acute stage, and the issue was steadily inflamed by the *Glasgow Free Press*, the polemics of which on behalf of alleged Irish grievances were indecently violent, anticipating the occasional journalistic excesses of the *Glasgow Observer* under its late editor. Nor were the Scottish clergy and laity sufficiently patient of the discipline of the vicars-apostolic. Strong diocesan government in Scotland was needed if the individualistic influence of the surrounding atmosphere of Presbyterianism was to be effectively checked.

The preliminary negotiations with Propaganda were spread over many years; but not until 1877, when it began to seem probable that the Holy See would take action, did these negotiations reach the practical stage. One of the main difficulties was the choice of the metropolitan see, for which Glasgow and Edinburgh contended, the former's claims supported by Cardinal Manning, those of the latter by Cardinal Wiseman.

In the end that time-honoured rivalry of the Middle Ages, which looked like beginning again, was allayed by uniting Edinburgh with St Andrews to give the easterly see a metropolitan dignity with the four suffragan sees of Aberdeen, Dunkeld, Galloway, and Argyll and the Isles, and erecting Glasgow into an archdiocese with suffragans, subject directly to the Holy See.

On March 4th, 1878, by the Bull *Ex Supremo Apostolatus Apice* Pope Leo XIII restored the hierarchy to Scotland.

The Papal announcement was received in Protestant Scotland with remarkable equanimity. No doubt the result of the restoration of the English hierarchy by Pius IX in 1850, after the crisis of hysteria it had caused, did not tempt the common sense of Scotsmen to a similar exhibition of nervous screaming. It had taken some discussion before it was finally settled to restore the titles of some of the pre-Reformation sees; but it was felt that the diplomatic reasons which had caused the restored English hierarchy to be given new episcopal titles did not apply in Scotland, where the Established Church was Presbyterian and where there were no cathedrals except ruins to mark visibly the appropriation by an established Church of ancient Catholic dioceses.

Nevertheless, one protest was made, and this was

by the Episcopalian body, based upon an astonishing claim of its bishops to " occupy by Divine permission the ancient sees of the Church of Scotland . . . and, whereas it is according to canonical rule and the order of the Catholic Church that there should be but one bishop in the same see, that the intrusion of a second bishop into a see already occupied is a violation of the law of unity, and a rending of the body of Christ."

With all the respect that is owed to a body of Christians whose members sacrificed everything to preserve an undeviating and passionate loyalty to their political founders, it is impossible to repress a melancholy smile at the muddled logic, inconsequential history, and peculiar theology which dictated that protest. Whatever future lies before the Episcopalian body must depend on its ability to represent in Scotland the Established Church of England with which it is in communion and from which it was no more than a cutting that failed to strike in Scottish soil.

Meanwhile, with the restoration of her hierarchy, the Catholic Church in Scotland, her strength of purpose invigorated, her confidence of its ultimate achievement secure, moved forward majestically but humbly under Almighty God on her Divine mission of restoring a nation to the full splendour of the Christian Faith.

CHAPTER VIII

IN the year 1872 the Established Church of Scotland surrendered all responsibility for the education of its youth to the State, and the State assumed the burden of compulsory education. Catholics, unable to contemplate the possibility of allowing their children to be exposed to the danger of the Protestant teaching of religion and history, continued to build and maintain their own schools, while at the same time rendering to Cæsar the things that were Cæsar's by payment of the education rate. What privations that responsibility cost the Catholic Church in Scotland may be imagined, for let it be remembered that the money not merely for every new school but for every new church had to be found from the pockets of Scottish Catholics, who are not remarkable for their great possessions. The result was an always harassing anxiety for the Catholic priests who had to beg the money, a cruel handicap for the Catholic teachers who had to accept lower salaries than the State-paid teachers, a grinding burden upon the Catholic parents of children, who had to find the money, and most serious of all, a grave material injustice to the Catholic children themselves, who were less well taught and less well housed than their little Protestant brothers and sisters, and who therefore entered the world at a marked disadvantage with them.

By the Scottish Education Act of 1918 the responsibility for Catholic schools was assumed by the State without prejudice to their Catholicism, and compensation was paid for the schools thus taken over. It was a progressive step which did honour to the Scottish nation and rendered a tardy justice which went some way to atone for the monstrous injustice of three centuries and a half. One likes to fancy that it was rendered through the sense of what was common in the Christianity of those who gave and those who received, that common Christianity of which the agony of the war had reminded them.

Whether it was due to the publication of those damning statistics that showed the catastrophic rate at which Scottish Presbyterianism was declining in numbers and influence, or whether to the early evidence of the social benefits which that Education Act had conferred on Scottish Catholicism, or whether merely to a dog in the Bethlehem manger lack of Christian charity, the Report of the Committee on Church Interests appointed by the General Assembly to consider (would it not have been more honest to say

" reconsider ? ") the 1918 Education Act is the most reactionary document to which any significant religious body has lent its prestige for many years, and although the Convener of that Committee is a Professor of Edinburgh University the Report itself betrays a degraded credulity and an unscrupulous assertiveness which recall the ebullitions of anonymous correspondents in the Scottish Press.

There is one recommendation the Committee makes which bears superficially the stamp of toleration; but when this is examined it turns out to be nothing better than a despicable surrender to the spirit of the age. " Let all religious tests for teachers be abolished," the Committee suggests, " except a religious test which will prevent any member of a religious order, male or female, from teaching in State schools."

Refuse the Sister of the Sacred Heart, refuse the Marist Brother, refuse the Benedictine whose founder was preserving Christianity a thousand years before the Established Church of Scotland was dreamed of, refuse the men and women whose lives have been dedicated exclusively to the service of Almighty God; but admit the psychological quack, admit the sexual faddist with his Freudian obsessions, admit the theophobe communist to corrupt with his godlessness the mind of Scottish youth, admit even Satan himself, who after all can cite Scripture to his purpose as well as John Knox and who can fairly be regarded as the first protestant of all.

Is the General Assembly really prepared to sacrifice Christianity altogether provided that by doing so it can secure itself against the contemplation of a time in the not too far distant future when Catholicism will mean Christianity, and Christianity Catholicism?

" What the future may have in store for the Church in Britain," wrote Principal W. M. Macgregor recently in *Life and Work*, " no one can predict, but in our country there is a rising tide of paganism both in faith and morals; and it is not inconceivable that some day all who call Jesus Lord may be driven to stand together, acknowledging and assisting one another, in order to save one nation from the deluge."

It would be unfair to deduce from these words that Principal Macgregor foresees the submission of all Presbyterians to the Catholic Church; but no Catholic can imagine any other possible way by which that fancy of his could be fulfilled. One may hope that Principal Macgregor's weighty rebuke to the organizers of the disgraceful mobs in Edinburgh in the year 1935 will have its effect.

" Sympathetic indignation is awakened and just-minded outsiders are driven to feel that, if Protestantism can be vindicated only in such crude ways, its day is nearly done."

It must be intolerably galling to a Presbyterian divine of his eminence that in the eyes of the indifferent or sceptical world the only contributions of news-value that Protestantism has been able to make to the history of this year of grace have been outbreaks of mob violence in Edinburgh, still more ferocious outbreaks of mob violence in Belfast, and a dispute between the members of a numerically negligible sect thrown off by one of the periodic disruptions of Presbyterianism whether dancing should be allowed at a children's party. And it must be intolerably galling to every member of the Established Church of Scotland to find the encouragement to fanaticism their own Assembly has given by the publication of that tragi-comic Report on Church interests embodied in a letter like that published on June 22nd, 1935, by the *Glasgow Weekly Herald*:

"A Reply to 'The Bailie'

" Sir,—In this weeks issue of the *Glasgow Weekly Herald*, I read an open letter to myself, The only point that appears to be open is the Absymal Ignorance of yourself, the writer. Firstly you state that after Mondays disgraceful proceedings, you do not want to know me, Well that is where your Mentality and mines differ, I like to come out in the open not to hide under a Nom-de-plume. Who are you anyway?

dictating lying and malicious statements and who are you speaking for? An open letter indeed! I did engineer as you term it, the proceedings, I did Protest, and Iam not ashamed of it all, let that sink Sir, I protested in the Usher Hall on behalf of the 100 per cent. Protestants in Britain and Australia, I have letters and a Cable from Australia advising me what to do with the save; the term Honoured, Guest, *Lyons he is hated there*, and the Scullin and Lyons, are known as the *White Ants, of Australia*, You question if many Edinburgh folks knew that Lyons was a papist? Every 100 per cent. Protestant knew, thats our mission in life to know our own business, I wish you knew the angles of your own job, I would not be answering to such vapourings, The High Constables who acted as Chuckers out should have been doing my job as they were brought into existence among other things, to repress Popery yet they asked me to leave when I was attempting to repress Popery, Sneeze Bailie your Brains are dusty, Criminals as a society have a right to existence but where? in Prison to prevent them carrying on with their criminal tactics to the detriment of Good Citizens, likewise R.C.'s, or, Papists, The doctrine they *must* believe pervents them giving an undivided loyalty, to our Protestant Throne. They are not even citizens, as a citizen is loyal, therefore we must not give them all the privlages of Citizenship, got that clear? Scotland does not want the good opinion of Lyons, or any other Papist, thats impossible unless Scotland goes Papist, and when the day comes along that I have to ask the craven unknown, Bailie, for advice, as to what Propaganda, is and how, to Propogate, my Protestant Principles, then I trust that that hole in Mother Earth will be open, waiting on my remains at least. I'll, be buried as John Cormack not under a Nom-de-Plume, Go Give Up the Ghost, Bailie, there are too many of your kind busying around. If you feel like it come to the Calton Hill or the Usher Hall on June 23 I will give you the *Great Unknown*, the chance to repeat your article verbally to that great audience.

JOHN CORMACK.
(Councillor)."

"*Editor's Note.*—Last week we published a protest against the outburst in the Usher Hall when the freedom of Edinburgh was being conferred on Mr Lyons, the Australian Premier. As the matter is of public importance the above letter by Councillor John Cormack is published without any attempt at sub-editing or punctuation. Editor, *Glasgow Weekly Herald.*"

Yet, unless the ministers and the members of the Established Church of Scotland make their disgust more evident, this Councillor of Edinburgh will succeed in turning the capital of their country into another Belfast. What that may mean will appear from the appeal sent by the Bishop of Down and Connor to the Prime Minister, Mr Baldwin, as lately as August 11th, 1935:

"DEAR SIR,—As Catholic Bishop of Down and Connor, I address you on behalf of the members of my afflicted flock, and I appeal to you, inasmuch as you are the present head of the Imperial Parliament who passed the Government of Ireland Act, 1920. . . . There is no religious equality in the Six Counties. Have Catholics any voice in legislation or any share in the administration, to which they are entitled? Do our Catholic youth, however great their ability, or whatever their qualifications, get their due proportion of public appointments? It is now well known that the name of the school or college where a boy receives his education is sufficient to debar him from a position. Have not our Catholic workers been expelled from their jobs and hunted from their homes? Have not our Catholic citizens, simply on account of their Catholicity, been terrorized and denied the very exercise of their civic rights, and made the victims by a state of affairs in this city of Belfast in which it would be difficult to find a parallel elsewhere.

"The attitude of the authorities in the Six Counties can be judged by their acts and speeches. The Prime Minister declared: 'Ours is a Protestant Government, and I am an Orangeman.' The Minister of Agriculture stated: 'I recommend people not to employ Roman Catholics, who are ninety-nine per cent. disloyal. . . .'

"The Executive have failed, and are failing, to maintain public order here in accordance with the provisions of the Government of Ireland Act, 1920. I need not multiply instances; let these two suffice. The brutal attacks on Catholic pilgrims while they were proceeding to the International Eucharistic Congress in Dublin in 1932 were so widely known and were so well remembered that it is unnecessary to describe them in detail. What measures did the Executive take to ensure the safety of Catholic citizens on that occasion; what steps did they take to bring the real culprits to justice? The present outbreak against Catholics in Belfast, extending over a period of months, has shocked all right-minded men, and has evoked a strong condemnation even from those of different religious belief both here and in England. Mobs have been permitted to hold possession of the streets, attacking Catholic people and their property, and congregating outside public works and demanding the suspension of Catholics; evictions, burnings; looting and intimidation have occurred in every part of the city; acts of a most un-Christian character have been perpetrated. Catholics have been compelled to fly for their lives in their night attire amongst the howls and jeers of the mob. A mother with her baby two days old was thrown into the street. Even ex-Servicemen have not been spared. They have been evicted from their homes and their furniture burned.

" And these incidents have occurred under the eyes of the armed forces of the Crown.

" The Committee formed to look after the victims has up to the present already checked 434 evicted families, comprising 1903 individuals, and the list is still uncompleted. On the 17th July I sent a telegram to Lord Craigavon urging him to take immediate steps to put an end to the un-Christian campaign that is now on foot to expel Catholic families from their homes. I got a brief acknowledgment, but the outrages continued. An extensive and carefully planned intimidation and victimization has taken place in the shipyards and at the docks. In the mills, factories and warehouses Catholic workers are denied the right to earn their livelihood. Yet, in the knowledge of these facts, the Prime Minister of Northern Ireland has reported to the Press on the 20th July, which then made the statement that the trouble in Belfast ' has never been so serious as has been made out.'

" The extent and gravity of this lawlessness cannot be allowed to be glossed over in this fashion. The causes of the present trouble are well known. The

Coroner of the City of Belfast, Mr T. E. Alexander, stated: 'The leaders of public opinion in high and responsible positions by their inflammatory speeches and enmity towards those differing from them in religion provoked and inflamed party passions, with the result that those breaches of the peace occurred.'

"Irish Catholics have a right—a right guaranteed to them by the Government of Ireland Act, 1920—to live in their native land and earn a livelihood in it. That right has been challenged. The present position is intolerable. A sworn inquiry before an impartial tribunal is imperative—a sworn inquiry into the nature, extent and causes of the outrages.

"On behalf of my flock I ask you to institute it. Appeals for an inquiry have been addressed to you by others, but have not, as far as I am aware, been fruitful. I am influenced by no political considerations. I write in my capacity as shepherd of my flock: I address you as the ultimate authority responsible for the Government of Ireland Act, 1920, under which the outrageous pogrom against my people has taken place. Whatever your answer may be, my Catholic people will put their trust in God, confident of the hope that the day will come when the seeds of suspicion and dissension, which are now being sown so assiduously by designing men for their own ends, will wither and die in the hands of those who scattered them."

We know only too well that the savage, nay, the sub-human bigotry of Orangemen is beyond calculation, and we know with equal certainty that such ferocity would never have been tolerated but for the base interest one political party has in fostering it with the hope of political advantage. It is difficult to free the mind of the suspicion that the Protestant agitations both in Belfast and Edinburgh have been systematically fed by the secret elements of that same political party. Yet to divert into dark foul channels the growing discontent of the Scottish people with their position in the world to-day, which is expressed on one side by a restless socialism rising to communism, on the other by a restless nationalism rising to the idea of complete separation from England, is a very dangerous method of drainage.

In a protest of the Archbishop of St Andrews and Edinburgh may be read the facts about Scotland. They are not pretty reading for the Committee set up to inquire into Church Interests, or for Mr Stanley Baldwin.

" The Eucharistic Congress which was recently held in Edinburgh has received more than normal prominence owing to the unreasoning storm of prejudice which for some months has been raging in the city.

" About the events of that week-end, much has been written and still more has been said. It is not my intention to deal with these statements in detail, but there is one side of the question to which I should like specially to direct attention.

" The Eucharistic Congress was purely a domestic concern affecting Catholics alone.

" No intimations regarding it were published in the non-Catholic press, and indeed—looking to the nature of the services and the meetings—the attendance of non-Catholics was not desired. In the choice of hall and site for the meetings we were guided merely by the necessity of supplying sufficient accommodation for the numbers expected to attend.

" In all possible respects we did our utmost to consider the feelings of non-Catholics.

" At the same time we claimed our right as citizens to meet in a public hall large enough to accommodate our members and to hold what functions we chose on our own property.

" The civic authorities fully recognized that right, and for their efforts during those troublous days we very cordially thank them.

" There are, however, many serious features in connection with the past few months with which the general public may not be entirely familiar but which are of the gravest concern to the welfare and peace of the community.

" For some months past Catholics have been sub-jected to a campaign of vilification, calumny and savagery that would be difficult to parallel in these days of enlightenment and progress.

"Not only has the Catholic Church been abused, misrepresented and slandered, but many of the most respected Catholic citizens have been calumniated and even accused of the most abominable crimes.

"The office which I have the honour to hold has been the object of gross insult and of the vilest accusations. For some time it has hardly been possible for a priest to appear in the city without being subjected to unspeakable indignities.

"They have been not only the target for vile abuse and most filthy and obscene language, but they have repeatedly been spat upon and molested in the public streets.

"In the factories and public works Catholic employees, and particularly defenceless girls, have suffered bitter persecution, as contemptible as it is cowardly, and strenuous efforts have been made to induce employers to dismiss Catholics on the ground of their religion alone.

"Furthermore, the shameful public events which have recently disfigured the fair name of Edinburgh are still fresh in the minds of all: the riotous tumult that welcomed the Catholic Young Men's Society at the City Chambers on the occasion of the civic reception and again on the Sunday at the Cathedral;

the further outburst at the Cathedral when the Catholics assembled to hold their thanksgiving service for the King on Jubilee Day; and the outrageous insult publicly offered to Mr Lyons, the Prime Minister of Australia.

" Yet these were but the prelude to the incredible outburst of insensate hate that was called forth by the Eucharistic Congress.

" Priests were savagely assaulted, elderly women attacked and kicked, bus-loads of children mercilessly stoned and inoffensive citizens abused and assailed in a manner that is almost unbelievable in any civilized community of to-day.

" During all this campaign of attack and persecution, the self-restraint of the Catholic body has been beyond all praise. In particular at the concluding service of the Congress, had that forbearance not been heroically sustained, bloodshed would undoubtedly have ensued.

" There are limits to human endurance, and, if the continuance of these conditions leads to dangerous public dispeace, then the disastrous consequences cannot be laid at the door of the Catholic body.

" The disgraceful scenes to which I have referred have become known in every quarter of the globe, and have sullied the fair name of a city which once was justly regarded as a leader in all culture, thought and civilization.

" It seems to me that the public of the capital of Scotland cannot regard such a result with equanimity. I am certain that the bulk of the citizens, fair-minded and enlightened as I know them to be, must, when the facts are brought to their knowledge, regard with abhorrence the actions of what, after all, is a mob of the lowest elements of the city, supported by importees of a similar class from other parts of the country.

" But the question which faces all who have the interests of the city at heart is—can this mob-rule be allowed to continue?

" It is undoubtedly the outcome of a campaign not merely of vilification and slander (which one could afford to ignore coming from the quarter it does) but of open and avowed incitement to riot and disorder. It is common knowledge that this campaign has been carried on for months in the public streets and halls of the city.

" In its latest phase its openly declared policy has been to prevent by unrestrained physical violence the attendance of law-abiding citizens at functions at which they are legitimately entitled to be present.

" If this campaign is allowed to continue we can only look for a continuance of the disgusting conduct of which I complain and for outbreaks of a more serious nature than those I have mentioned.

" It is for responsible citizens and for those to

whom the maintenance of peace and order in the community is committed to say whether they are to court a repetition of those regrettable outbursts of mob fury which have disgraced the city in the eyes of the world in recent months or to take effectual steps to prevent them.

" I leave it there for the present."

To this protest Councillor Cormack, presumably after taking advice from one of his partially literate assistants, has thus replied :

" This country is regarded as the key to Protestantism and it was unwise, to say the least, that you should have entertained even the thought of a Eucharistic Congress in this country, especially in the capital city.

" Efforts have been made to induce employers to dismiss Catholics, and I am going all out to carry this still further.

" The campaign has only just started, but will soon be on its way, especially when next November comes and I have a few more Protestant Councillors in the City Chambers.

" Then the following November when I have a majority you and your ilk will realize what real Protestant Action means." [1]

The promised excesses are some weeks away while

[1] This threat was nullified by the result of the municipal elections.

these words are being written, and the licence which
the civic authorities of Edinburgh are prepared to
extend to their urbane and cultured colleague is not
yet known. Meanwhile, Catholics await from the
ecclesiastical authorities an official condemnation of
the outrages already committed and the smallest sign
of a genuine effort to avert the graver disorders
threatened for the future.

The embittered religious feeling is still further
embittered by the habit anti-Catholics have of
identifying Catholicism in Scotland with the Irish
population. It is apparently not realized by these
good Presbyterians (and until we receive an official
contradiction we are bound to assume that the riff-
raff of Edinburgh does consist of good Presbyterians)
that immigration from Ireland has practically ceased
and that many more English now enter Scotland every
year to take up well-paid permanent jobs, than Irish
to seek the miserable wages by which their Scottish
employers once lured them from the sharper misery
of an Ireland that was still unfree. If the Scots who
lament so woefully the Irish incubus seriously wish
to be rid of it, why do they not try to effect an exchange
between the Catholics of Glasgow and the Protestants
of Ulster? Those Protestants who for no other
purpose than material gain aggravate with the con-
nivance of English politicians a festering sore on the

body of Ireland. The Irish nation is faced by a much more difficult Scottish problem than the Irish problem which vexes Scotland.

It may be true that the Irish in Scotland have conserved their nationality and in conserving it remained aliens in the country of their adoption. But whose is the chief blame for that? They fled from famine and persecution to be greeted with commercial exploitation and ostracism, and for as many as four generations they have been treated as aliens, and heathen aliens too. In writing that, there is no suggestion of accepting the problem of assimilation as insoluble. No wiser move towards its solution was made than the Education Act of 1918, and if the relief thus granted to Catholics be not grudged from jealousy of the freedom it has given to extend their religious influence by building much-needed churches, the complete assimilation of the Irish element into the material life of their adopted country will proceed apace. None desires this more ardently than the Scottish Catholics, and nothing makes their relations with their Scoto-Irish brethren more difficult than these outbursts of shameful bigotry.

The accusation of divided loyalty is one that is continuously levelled against all Catholics. We are faintly surprised to find that the motto of the Protestant Action Society, of which that *preux chevalier*, Mr

Cormack, is organizing secretary, is "Liberty and Justice." That motto is elegantly amplified beneath with this announcement: "We do not proscribe a Romanist in politics because of his religion, but because his religion makes it impossible to loyally serve his country when the civil law conflicts with the ecclesiastical. Do you get that?"

Should the civil law ever conflict with the laws of God, Catholics will undoubtedly yield their allegiance to the laws of God, and we may surely suppose that every good Protestant would follow the same course. The existence of any ecclesiastical law which conflicts with the civil law of Scotland is unknown to Catholics.

The question of a divided loyalty of sentiment is another matter. The Irish who settled in Scotland settled in a country which seemed to them to have surrendered what they had never surrendered— nationhood. Scotland represented to them as it represents to most of the rest of the world to-day an extension of England. They were not willing to suffer a comparable loss of status, and finding where they penetrated little peculiarly Scottish left except religious intolerance and sectarian hate, they preferred to remain expatriate Irish. During the end of the nineteenth and the beginning of the twentieth century the tendency of conventional Presbyterianism to decline into a mild form of deism, save where as in the more recently evangelized Highlands and Islands a gloomy fervour of a sort persisted was symptomatic of the decline of Scotland as a whole into a provincial unimportance. Now, the Catholic Church requires something larger than a provincial background if she is to give a nation the chance to express its peculiarly national Catholicism. Hence what began to look like the rapid absorption of Scottish Catholicism into Irish Catholicism, against which Blessed Oliver Plunket had warned Rome in the seventeenth century. It was humiliating for Scottish Catholics to find St Andrew's Day removed from the list of holidays of obligation and St Patrick's Day only not a holiday of obligation through what may without irreverence be called the ruse of making St Joseph's Day one.

Yet, when at long last there were signs of a national reawakening, the Scoto-Irish students of Glasgow University were in the van of that movement to restore to Scotland her integrity, so prominently indeed that the whole National Party of Scotland was believed by many to be no better than a sinister agent of Popery. Anxious to deodorize itself of the combined reek of incense and gunpowder the National Party allowed a motion demanding the repeal of the 1918 Education Act to be moved by the Secretary of the Party at the annual conference. It is true that the motion was talked out, but it was made evident to Nationalists who were also Catholics that the restoration to Scotland of her status as a sovereign nation might mean simultaneously the restoration of that spirit of religious violence, infection by which had first led the way to the destruction of Scotland's nationhood.

For every Catholic Nationalist the problem of divided loyalty became acute, and the fruit of it was visible in the result of the Glasgow Rectorial election of 1934. Even national independence can be achieved at too dear a price if such independence is to mean a recession along the dim and tortuous paths of religious bigotry. Remove from the pages of Scottish history those written with the blood of Scottish Catholics, and how pale that history will be! Obliterate from the annals of patriotism the names of Malcolm Canmore, of Alexander III, of Wallace, of Bruce, of Andrew of Moray, of Bishop Wishart and Bishop Lamberton, of Cardinal Beaton, of Mary, Queen of Scots, of Prince Charles Edward Stuart, and would not these annals seem a little thin afterwards? Yet, rather than help in any way by word, or action the re-creation of a sovereign Scotland in which the old religious hatreds were re-created with it, the Scottish Catholic would prefer to admit that his glorious patriotic past is irrevocable in the present. The blame would rest on the country which rejected him, on the country which esteemed higher the preservation of her little Established Kirk at the cost of injustice to her 600,000 Catholics, *all* of whom would be the most loyal Scots in a Scotland that was *herself* again. Fortunately for his peace of mind, the Scottish Catholic knows that he can do his country no richer service than to devote all his energy, all his emotion, all his eloquence to upholding and spreading what he believes to be the only Truth that can guide man safely towards his immortal destiny. The Real Presence of God upon her altars will be more precious to Scotland than the real presence of a Parliament in Edinburgh. The Scottish Catholic can afford to forget Bannockburn, will repine no more at Flodden or Pinkie Cleugh, and may count even Culloden well lost, if he remind himself that no country's independence is worth winning unless it be won for the dedication of it to the greater glory of God.